REVIEWS FOR

SLAYIN' SINGLEHOOD:

Janice Rigel has written a timeless novel of encouragement for anyone who has felt disappointment in their season. Read this book - and learn the richness that God has in store for your life as you 'slay single-hood and beyond.

—**Anna Pranger,** Co-Founder of *Stirred Up Ministries.*

***

Slayin' Singlehood was such a wonderful and impactful read! Within the first few minutes I already knew two things; 1 - I wouldn't be able to put this book down, and 2 - It was time for me to delete my dating apps...again.

—**Briana Richardson,** Songwriter and Worship Leader at *Stirred Up Ministries.*

***

Janice puts a whole new spin on the popular phrase "Slay All Day". In "Slayin' Singlehood" Janice teaches us to "Slay Every Season" and find power, purpose, and fulfilment in a waiting season. This book is for anyone who needs encouragement during a time of pressing in for the promises that God has for you! While I am not single, I was able to hold onto the truths of God's word that Janice presented to help me in my season of waiting on the Lord in my career.

—**Lindsay Kudritz,** Teacher.

***

Slayin' Singlehood is rich with wisdom and insights only obtained by forging through one's pain and heartache. Janice's documented journey through healing from her divorce and subsequent joy-finding apply not only to singles but to anyone who has the pain to overcome or feels as if they are waiting on God to work in their life. Through funny anecdotes, incredible stories of faith, and a multitude of scripture references, Slayin' Singlehood will inspire the single person--as well as the not-single person--to go deeper with the God of healing and promise.

-Janelle James, Founder of *TransitionWell Consulting, LLC.*

***

Compelling. Inspiring. Captivating. So many words could describe 'Slayin' Singlehood'. A strong message of hope and redemption that this generation needs to hear can be found within the pages of this book. With meaningful and humorous stories from Janice's life and the Bible splashed throughout the book, you will be encouraged and challenged by Slayin' Singlehood. The only difficult thing will be putting it down once you start reading!

-Cindy Eckhart, Founder of *One Step Ministries and Field Manager with Break the Grey Ministries.*

***

I didn't know Janice in her married life, but it is evident that God is real and alive in her single life. Seeing her life now it is obvious that she is an overcomer, by the blood of the Lamb and the word of her testimony (Revelation 12:11). Whoever she decides to marry will be blessed beyond words.

-Deb Wasnich, Prayer Warrior.

SLAYIN' SINGLEHOOD:

Celebrating Life in Every Season

JANICE RIGEL

Published by KHARIS PUBLISHING, an imprint of KHARIS MEDIA
LLC.

Copyright © 2021 Janice Rigel

ISBN-13: 978-1-946277-82-4
ISBN-10: 1-946277-82-7

Library of Congress Control Number: 2020952118

Cover image: Anna Pranger

All KHARIS PUBLISHING products are available at special quantity
discounts for bulk purchase for sales promotions, premiums, fundraising, and educational needs. For details, contact:

Kharis Media LLC
Tel: 1-479-599-8657
support@kharispublishing.com
www.kharispublishing.com

KHARIS
PUBLISHING

Dedication

I dedicate this book to my two namesakes, Janice Ann and Carol Louise, affectionately known as my Grandmas. They inspired me to write from an early age and I know both of them are cheering me on from Heaven. Because of them, my life has been filled with happy memories that I will cherish forever and it is my joy to carry on their legacies in all that I do.

CONTENTS

Foreword

Slayin' Singlehood. Friends, you need this book in your life! It's something we all need to embrace, but it's one of the things we fight the hardest. The name stands out all on its own, and the truth inside of it will change your life. From beginning to end Janice helps you truly pinpoint where you're at in your journey, and allows you to find joy in celebrating that moment.

The message behind her words shows us how to embrace every season of our life in order to truly find healing and growth. I find the truth behind it is that you can never assess your future unless you address your now. The enemy wants nothing more than to keep you bound to painful memories of yesterday so that you don't find purpose in this moment today. He does that by keeping your mind focused on the issue so that you don't discover the answer! Slayin' Singlehood helps you discover that the answer is not only in Christ, but it's in your ability to celebrate the seasons of change.

It's so easy to blame our brokenness, pain, and lack of growth on other people and the circumstances in our life. Through it all I've discovered that the breaking may not be my fault, but the building is my responsibility. How silly would it be to stay stuck in the rubble of yesterday when there is so much beauty to be built right now? Friend, Jesus takes us through seasons not to punish us, but to position us for more. You may be experiencing all the different seasons of life, but you are being taught how to get rid of weeds, plant yourself in Him, wait while being watered, and how to grow so that you are ready when the time comes!

With every chapter Janice uncovers the beauty behind the process of singleness while celebrating every season along the way. I love how real she is with her story as she opens up about how hard the journey can truly be while not allowing us to stay in a place of desperation. I feel her heart in every chapter, and can relate to her story in a way that makes me feel hope and peace for those who will grab ahold of her words. I'm so proud of her and am honored to be writing this foreword for her book. Thank you for being obedient and raw with us as you poured your heart into these pages. I can't wait to see the freedom that transpires when people read your words! I'm so proud of you for unapologetically sharing your heart, and allowing us to find healing from your story.

So much love,

Alissa Holt.

Chapter One

Seasons

To everything there is a season, and a time for every purpose under heaven. —Ecclesiastes 3:1

Life is lived in seasons unraveled by time and the unfolding of God's purposes and plans. Some seasons are seemingly short and gone in the blink of an eye, while others feel never-ending, as if they will last forever and a few days. Some seasons are stamped with happy memories, fulfilled promises, and exceedingly met expectations, while others are marked with mystery, question marks, pain, and heartache.

Ecclesiastes sings the song of the soul traveling through uncharted territory, eternally reminding us that He has a plan and purpose for every season under heaven. That includes the sometimes taboo and usually undesirable season many try so hard to run through as rapidly as possible, or to slide past altogether: singlehood!

Navigating through a season of singleness with wisdom, intentionality, and purpose not only honors the Lord, but it also ensures that the season God has you in is not wasted. I believe that nothing with God is ever wasted when we willingly surrender it to Him and allow His plans and purposes to unfold in the beautiful way that He designed them.

Romans 8:28 tells us that God works all things together for the good of those who love Him and are called according to His purpose. Because I believe that all scripture is inspired by God and is true, I can stand on this verse (and all others) and believe it for myself. You can do the same!

If you are in a season of singleness, don't cheapen or discount it. If you know someone who is currently navigating through singlehood, don't push them through or devalue the season where God has placed them. There is a deep richness and value in the season of singlehood

1

that, sadly, most never find. So, don't look at singlehood like a clearance item that you find on a shelf at the back of the store that no one wants and is hard to sell even with a slashed price. Instead, look at singlehood as a rare treasure that you would only find in an upscale store, locked in a beautiful glass case, monitored closely with surveillance, and surrounded by security. That's a much better depiction of singlehood.

Different seasons call for different attire. Sometimes you need a coat, sometimes you can go sleeveless, and sometimes you need a rain poncho. I live in Michigan and all three of these could be worn in the span of one day! One thing I have learned about myself in my single season is that I LOVE fashion (if only my budget matched that love). As a woman of God, I want to always dress for the occasion called "life" and represent Him well. In every season, we can wear the same beautiful attire as the noble woman described in Proverbs 31: strength, honor, and dignity. Colossians 3:12 adds compassion, kindness, humility, gentleness, and patience to our spiritual wardrobe. It may sound like an expensive wardrobe, but the beautiful thing is that Jesus paid the price for this wardrobe and gives us the ability to wear all of these things, every day and in every season.

Relationship status has become a big part of our identity as a culture. It's one of the first things we talk about when we meet new people, and one of the few shallow ways we describe ourselves on social media.

I am no exception to the unspoken cultural expectation to be in a relationship. At fifteen years old, I began what I call my first "real" relationship with a guy. By that, I mean it was the first guy I liked who actually reciprocated the same feelings. Although I was not allowed to date until I was sixteen, I enjoyed all of the benefits of a relationship while I waited for my birthday without an official "girlfriend" title. We talked on the phone daily for hours, went on "unofficial" dates to the movies and karaoke, and shared our affections by means of handholding, kissing, and "I love you's." Nothing more physical happened in this relationship. Several months passed and the long-awaited arrival of my "Sweet Sixteen" birthday was met with an abrupt end to that so-called relationship (if you could even call it that). For no good reason, he stopped calling and coming around. Not surprisingly, I did hear rumors that he started seeing someone else. I was disappointed and heartbroken but moved on with my life, mostly because I had no other option.

Not many months later, I was introduced to someone through some mutual friends. We seemed to hit it off quickly. As a girl without much experience in the realm of romantic relationships, it felt refreshing and reaffirming to have another guy take an interest in me. It was even more exciting that I could actually officially date because I had met the age requirement established by my parents! At the time, I can honestly say my standards for a relationship were non-existent and consisted of nothing more than two things: a person of the opposite sex and someone who was interested in me. The idea of examining someone's character, faith, and life ambitions was the furthest thing from my mind, because I hadn't gone deeply into any of those in my own life.

I dated him for approximately six months. We did all of the normal things teenage dating couples do. We talked for hours on the phone, hung out every chance we could get, went to the movies, and even went to an amusement park together. Very quickly, he confessed his love for me, and I gladly accepted and reciprocated my confession of love for him. Our physical relationship never went further than holding hands and bird-like kisses (pecks), which did not fulfill his hormone-raged expectations. Because I was unwilling to be physical, that relationship ended when he found someone who would comply with what he was looking for. Even though I am eternally grateful for the end of that very shallow relationship, at the time it was very painful and hurt me deeply. Like Real Talk Kim says, "heartbreak ain't no joke." Rejection is never easy in the moment, even when it turns out to be God's way of protecting us.

I will never forget the night that I found out he had cheated on me. We all have those moments and memories, especially when it involves trauma, where details are etched in your mind like a tattoo artist permanently inking someone's skin. I could not sleep as I tossed and turned with unrelenting tears pouring down my face. Finally, around two a.m., I attempted to escape the trapping pain I felt within the unsympathetic, bright pink walls of my bedroom. I slipped quietly out of my house, wrapped like a burrito in my big blanket. With my heavy heart, I tromped through my backyard and laid down on the somewhat damp trampoline, breathing in the fresh summer air, and feeling some relief solely in the change of scenery. After a short time, I became unsettled and uncomfortable and decided to relocate to the porch swing in my front yard.

On that creaky swing, I did something I had not done in a very long time: I prayed. I prayed to the God I had heard and learned about in my younger years of Sunday school and Vacation Bible School. This was the God that I really did not know personally; but the ache in my soul that night drew out a desire to call out to Him in a real and personal way. I knew I needed Him, and I needed Him desperately. I had sought to find my value and fulfillment in relationships, which ended in heartache and deep disappointment. I don't remember exactly what I prayed that night, but I do know that God met me where I was, like He does with all of us. That summer night was a pivotal night for me. It set my life on a completely different trajectory and, more than sixteen years later, I am still marked by that middle-of-the-night encounter with my Creator.

The next fall, I entered my junior year of high school "single." That wasn't necessarily my preference or choice, though. It was mostly due to the fact that when you're from a small town, you've grown up with your opposite-gender classmates, and they become more like siblings than dating material. At least that's how it was for me.

I very much enjoyed the school year with my friends, attended my first prom with "my girls," and even took on a role in the one and only musical that was put on during my high school years," He Ain't Done Right by Nell." I love my small town, but opportunities were sporadic and limited. By participating in the play, I discovered a passion and love for performance and made new friends that were outside of my junior class.

During the springtime of my junior year, I attended my school's track and field invitational. Those that know me are probably turning their heads sideways and wondering why, because they understand how unusual it is for me to attend any athletic events. Those that don't know me may not think it sounds like a big deal, but I assure you that my non-athletic self does not normally do things like that. To illustrate my point, I played softball one summer in sixth grade, and that was only because my uncle was the coach. I once caught the ball in the outfield and had no idea that I was supposed to throw it back in. The crowd burst out in an uproar of laughter, as I jumped up and down, squealing and celebrating the fact that somehow the ball landed in my mitt, while my uncle yelled for me to throw it in—oops! I also hit my friend in the face with a softball during warmup and left a giant knot on her forehead. In middle school, most of my lunch break recess time was spent inside playing foosball. My lack of interest in the physical activity that the outdoors offered led me to settle for this second-best option so I could stay inside. One time I managed to knock my friend in the face with the foosball handle. I'm not entirely sure it was my fault, but it did happen.

Then there were times of being hit in the face with a kickball during gym class, as I ran to first base (I was always too slow and never made it on base), getting yelled at for talking to my best friend at the goalie box, and not moving during soccer. Also, my mom had to write notes excusing me from activities that involved running because I had asthma.

I joined the cheerleading squad during the basketball season of my freshman year, only because I am loud and there weren't cuts. I cannot do a cartwheel, and my attempt to do the splits ended with a ripped pair of pants. I even mistakenly wore my body suit on the *outside* of my bloomers--and yes, someone noticed when I did a jump at a game and let me know about it.

I've never had strong athletic abilities, or a desire to be athletic for that matter, so my attendance at the track invitational that spring was way out of the norm for me. I had never gone to one before, nor have I gone to one since. But God had a purpose for it.

I met someone there and, because I met him, my life changed forever. Remember that musical I was in? Well, there was someone in the cast who was two classes below me, and I really wanted to reconnect with him. This was before social media made connections and reconnections easier. I found someone who I thought may know him, and sure enough he did. A big hooray for small schools! I was able to quickly get his phone number, and I returned to socializing with my friends. I had no intention of talking to the guy who gave me the phone number again.

My socializing for the night ended too early when all of my friends had to go home. I decided to stay and, since I had no friends there, I found the guy who gave me the phone number earlier and hung out with him. I did most of the talking (shocker) and wondered what was going on in his mind, because he sure didn't say much. He was incredibly shy and backward, which I found more intriguing than attractive.

That awkward and curious evening together sparked a friendship that lasted for over ten years. After a few months of talking and spending a lot of time together, he asked me out and, without hesitation, I said yes. He was a church boy, and I found that very interesting and appealing. He was definitely a different type of guy than the two I had dated prior to him. We would talk for hours every evening on the phone (yes, he finally did start talking). Every Wednesday when I called, his mom would tell me he was at youth group. It didn't take long for me to invite myself, and I started attending church with him.

Within a few months, I had a real encounter with the same God whom I had prayed to on that summer night a year prior. I realized the enormity of my sin and the reason I truly needed a Savior. I surrendered my life to the One who created it in the first place--Jesus Christ. I was baptized and began a real relationship with Him. I was hungry for more of God, to know His Word (the Bible), to pray, and to seek after all the ways to fully integrate God in my life.

My relationship with my boyfriend continued and, four years after we began dating, we were married. I loved and cared about him deeply, and so I knowingly overlooked many obvious signs that I should have ended the relationship before it ever got to the point of us standing at an altar together, making vows before God and our family and friends.

My life was wrapped up in him. I felt trapped and stuck in the relationship and didn't see a way out prior to marriage. I tried to end it a few times while we were dating, but my attempts were always unsuccessful, and I was lured back in by shallow promises, empty commitments, and guilt trips. Hindsight really is 20/20.

After seven years of marriage and much heartache, sprinkled with some good times as well, our marriage ended because of an affair. So that makes one hundred percent of the few relationships I've had complete failures, and all for the same reason. This time, though, I had something I didn't have during my other two breakups--a relationship with God. That alone sustained me through the difficult, heartbreaking, unexpected, and unwanted journey of divorce and brought me deep healing and freedom (more on those good things later).

Now I am writing to you as a woman in her early thirties, still journeying through my season of singlehood with a heart full of joy and expectation for the good things that have taken place and those yet to come. I have had to wrestle and tear down countless strongholds and lies, as I have adamantly pursued wholeness in all areas of my life. I have found victory and continue to claim it for myself, and I am believing and claiming the same for you.

This season is not for the faint of heart. It is not easy at all. But it is so full of God's immense love, enormous goodness, unchanging faithfulness, and beautiful treasures. You can find these too, if you'll simply look for them.

I echo again the words of Ecclesiastes: there is a purpose for this season. Whether you want to be sure you get the most out of your season of singleness, or you want to know how to relate and offer empathy to a sing someone you know, I pray that this book is a source of wisdom, encouragement, and a beacon of light for you. Blessings to you as we navigate this journey together, discover the plans and purposes of God in it, and make the absolute most out of the single season.

Chapter Two

Heal the Hurt

He heals the brokenhearted and binds up their wounds —Psalms 147:3

Life isn't always mountaintops, sunshine, rainbows, and butterflies, although I would be happy if this was true. My ideal world would be filled with sparkly moments, laughter, dancing, and unlimited Reese's cups. I would love it if it only rained colorful confetti, and the wind blew our best wishes into fruition, but in a fallen world that isn't reality. There are hurtful and unfair experiences on our life path, where we are forced to navigate and trudge through valleys, trenches, and potholes so deep they'll knock the fender off of your car (hello Michigan backroads). Even in the most unfair and undeserving circumstances, we never have to adopt a victim mindset. There is always victory, healing, and freedom for us that is found in Christ.

Stuffing away emotions and feelings, trying to hide them and move on from the pains of life, pretending hurtful things did not really happen or minimizing them, sometimes feels like the best, and even only, option. I can say this because I've done those very things more than I care to admit. The sad reality is that traumas don't just go away on their own. Past pain and heartbreak will inevitably show itself in other areas of life unless, or until, we face and deal with them. I want to encourage you to take time during this chapter to let God heal anything from your past that may hinder your daily life and the health of potential future relationships (both platonic and romantic). Jeremiah 17:14 declares a truth that I want to share with you: "O Lord, if you heal me, I will be truly healed." He is our source of victory, healing, and freedom. He is the remedy for every hurt that needs healing.

I also want to tell you that you can be happy, healthy, and whole in every area of your life. This is something we often don't believe, but it's the truth. One of the most beautiful names for Jesus is *Prince of Peace*. The Hebrew word for peace is *shalom*. Shalom has such deep, rich meaning and is a beautiful gift God gives His people. (see Psalms 29:11) Besides peace, shalom means harmony, wholeness, completeness, prosperity, welfare, and tranquility. I believe that God wants shalom, His perfect wholeness, for every area of your life.

Rejection is ugly and painful. It can make us question our self-worth and believe that we are flawed, unworthy, and not good enough. I dealt with rejection from all of my crushes during my school years, as well as betrayal in the few serious relationships I've had. Either they did not reciprocate the same feelings or, as I shared earlier, commitment was always contingent and short-lived. It would be easy for me to use my past experiences as an excuse to create untrue stereotypes about all men. I could build unhealthy walls around my heart and shut myself away from the idea of a romantic relationship out of fear of broken trust and being hurt again. But that is not, and will not be, my story.

The past few years have been a journey of intentionally seeking God for healing. I do desire to be in a healthy, godly relationship someday, and fully believe it's part of God's plan for my life. I want to be sure I am healed and ready when that time comes but, even more than that, I want to walk in total healing because I want to be whole for myself. I want to enjoy my life and all that God has for me without unnecessarily dragging along pain from my past.

Another name for God is *Jehovah Rapha*, which means "the God who heals" or "the Lord that heals.[1] " During the process of my divorce, I ripped out a page from one of my many journals and wrote Jehovah Rapha and stuck it on the front of my refrigerator. I needed a physical and frequent reminder that God is my healer.

The Bible is full of stories of how God heals His people physically, emotionally, mentally, and spiritually. There is no limit to the ways He heals. The first mention of Jehovah Rapha is found in the Old Testament book of Exodus. God declares Himself as "the Lord, who heals you" in response to a miracle He performed for the Israelites. They had been freed from slavery in Egypt and were trekking through the

---

[1] https://www.christianity.com/wiki/god/what-does-it-mean-that-god-is-jehovah-rapha.html

desert en route to the Promised Land God was giving them.

They had traveled three days without finding any water. My "modern day self" can hardly imagine a few days without Pepsi, let alone water deprivation in a desert. When they finally did find water, it was bitter. God performed a miracle by providing a piece of wood for Moses to throw into the water, making it fit to drink. He then instructed them to listen carefully and do right in His eyes and, in return, He promised to keep them from the diseases the Egyptians had experienced. Instruction and promise on top of healing--He is so good! That was the moment He first revealed Himself as the God who heals; but healing didn't start and stop with the Israelites in the wilderness.

All throughout Scripture we can read accounts of how God healed people. Skip ahead to the New Testament and read through the first four books (Matthew, Mark, Luke, and John), also known as the Gospel accounts. They document wonderfully the life of Jesus and His ministry on earth. He healed the lame and the lepers, restored sight to the blind, set people free from unclean spirits, and so much more.

One woman who suffered with menstrual bleeding for twelve years had exhausted all of her resources on doctors, but her condition only grew worse. When she encountered Jesus and touched the hem of His outer garment, she was healed in an instant. Another man who was blind since birth had his own healing encounter. Jesus made mud out of a mixture of his spit and some dirt, put it on the man's eyes, and told him to go rinse it off in a pool. The man received his sight. God is completely unconventional and unpredictable in His methods, always deserving of glory and leaving no room for us to credit anyone else.

I love knowing that the accounts of healing we read in the Bible are not even close to being all-inclusive. John 21:25 tells us that Jesus did so many miracles that all of the books in the world could not even contain them--and He is still healing and setting people free today!

A few years back, I contracted a horrible staph infection on my left leg. What started as a painful sore turned into a gross, gaping hole about the size of a quarter, which needed serious medical attention. For about three months, I had weekly appointments at a wound clinic. It was very painful, inconvenient, and costly. My appointments always consisted of waiting in a room for twenty minutes after the doctor put a glob of numbing gel on the infection. Then the doctor would come in, usually with an assistant and, for lack of actual medical verbiage, do some sort of scraping and prodding in an attempt to stimulate healing and cell growth. I had to take ibuprofen each time so that, when the numbing wore off, the pain from the treatment would be bearable. At every appointment pictures and measurements were taken to document and track my progress.

On top of my in-office treatment, I was also given medication and home treatments. Thank God one of my good friends also had a nurse's heart and helped me with my home treatments, which consisted of medicating and packing the sore spot. Yeah, not fun. Throughout the few months of treatment, my progress of healing was slow at best, and more often stagnant. It was frustrating seeing little to no signs of improvement week after week.

My most difficult appointment was when the doctor reported that my infection had not only shown no improvement but had in fact gotten worse. She named the new infection, confirmed by lab results, (which I don't remember and probably couldn't spell even if I did), and let me know that my only option for treatment was IV therapy, which required hospitalization. She also let me know that it was an extremely painful procedure, and that my insurance would not cover any of the $20,000 cost.

My intense feelings of frustration and self-pity were quickly trampled by an even greater desire and will to pray and believe in God for my healing. I can honestly say that up until I received that disappointing diagnosis, I hadn't even considered praying for healing. I am thankful for the doctors and the health profession and expected a medical route to resolve my infection issue, but that wasn't working.

I called together a group of my close friends to pray for me, and we met within the next few days. They came to my house, gathered around me, and prayed for God to heal my leg. During that time of prayer, I know I received what 1 Corinthians 12 refers to as the gift of faith. I had no doubt in my mind whatsoever that God could and would heal my leg. I saw no other options and, after months of seeing the very best wound doctors, I had only grown worse--much like the woman in the Gospel with the issue of blood.

When I returned to the wound clinic the next week, the doctor was astonished and happy to tell me that my leg had no trace of infection.

While I was very happy hearing her confirm my healing, I was not at all astonished or surprised at the news. I fully expected and believed, before my appointment, that God had completely healed me. She requested that I follow-up with a specialist to confirm it, but said that I would have no reason to return to her office. I was released from her care that day. I kept my appointment with the specialist, who did confirm that I had no infection in my leg. I let him know that my friends had prayed for me, and Jesus had healed my leg. He smiled and told me that he sees God heal many people on the medical mission trips he takes. Before I left the office, he asked to pray for me, which was the best way to end the crazy infection story and celebrate my healing. This is such a fun story to tell, and it has fueled my faith to believe in God for more healings in my own life and the lives of others.

One morning while I was getting ready for the day, severe pain began surging through my foot. Because I had former issues with this foot where I had to get steroid shots, take medication, and wear a boot, I immediately started racking my brain for how I could fit a doctor's appointment into my week and repeat the process I had before. Then I thought to pray first. I picked up my foot with both hands and prayed for God to heal it. It was a simple prayer, and the pain left immediately. I haven't had an issue with it since.

I was diagnosed with PCOS (Polycystic Ovary Syndrome) a few years ago and had very irregular menstrual cycles. I decided to refuse the long-term medication and started seeking God for healing. One evening I was watching Nate Johnston do a live video on social media and, as he was praying, he said, "Someone watching right now has been diagnosed with PCOS and God wants to heal you.[2]" That is what the 1 Corinthians 12 calls a word of knowledge. I simply said, "I receive that," and since that time I have had regular periods and believe that God healed me.

My stories are a drop in the ocean of healing testimonies that exist. He will never run out of ability or willingness to heal His creation. So I pray right now that if you are in need of healing, you apply your faith with mine and receive the healing God has for you. I believe God wants to heal you! I don't believe a cookie-cutter prayer or method for healing exists. I believe we simply just have to ask and receive, like the

---

[2] Johnston, N. (Date?) Everyday Revivalists. Retrieved from https:// www.nateandchristy.co

Bible says.

God's healing is not limited to just physical. He also can heal us emotionally and mentally. I felt such intense heartache from my broken marriage, that I could tangibly feel pain in the depths of my innermost being. The betrayal of adultery constantly consumed my thoughts, tormenting most of my waking moments. I couldn't seem to escape the reality of my situation, and it felt impossible to think of anything other than my aching heart. My mind always felt foggy, and I had a difficult time even thinking a clear thought, let alone verbalizing much that made sense. I specifically remember someone asking me what I do at my job. I was so embarrassed because, even though I spent forty hours a week at my place of employment and had been there a few years, my mind went completely blank. I managed to mutter a jumbled answer and divert the conversation to something else.

There are so many vices that we can use to numb our pain, but they are like cheap band-aids on a festering wound. I didn't want a quick, short-lived fix that would wear off and immediately confront me again with the reality of my brokenness. I wanted real, lasting healing, and my remedy was prayer and worship. I was very serious about pursuing God-given healing and wholeness.

In the months following my separation, I spent many evenings alone seeking God in my living room with YouTube worship music playing on my TV. I would lay hands on my own head and declare healing over my mind and ask God to heal my broken heart. He would tell me, "just let Me love you." Many times "letting Him love me" means playing worship music and lying still as the truth-filled lyrics and His presence wash over me. It's important to know and remind ourselves that we don't have to work for God's love, grace, and mercy; we simply have to receive it.

I prayed fervently and believed for the "head fog" to lift. On my way to work one morning, it finally did. As my car reached the top of a hill while travelling my usual route, a beautiful, bright sunrise danced across my windshield and, in that moment, I felt the heaviness of my broken heart lift off me, and the fog from my mind dissipated in an instant. For the first time in a long time, I began to think and speak clearly, and my mind was no longer constantly consumed with my pain.

Through renewing my mind with the Word, listening to messages from some of my favorite preachers, going to Him in prayer, and basking in His presence with worship music, God did heal my broken heart. I don't hurt anymore from the broken relationships in my past. If He did it for me, He can do it for anyone. He never stops healing His people because He is good, and He loves us deeply. I encourage you to reach out to God and let Him love you, and keep loving you, too.

I did not want to carry any baggage from my past into my future. I knew God had the ability and was willing to help me go through those proverbial bags and deal with whatever was inside, so I allowed Him to. He helped me trash the ugly contents (lies and faulty mindsets), while revealing more of Himself, His love, and the truth to me in the process.

One of the best gifts God has given me during my single season has been good, quality friendships. They have spoken bold truth into my life, helping me uproot lies the enemy tried to plant in my heart and mind--the lies of not being good enough, being too much, and everything in-between. God's truth always trumps every lie. My friends have helped me heal so much and have also been there for times of uncontrollable laughs, coffee dates, road trips, and late-night phone calls. Friendships are the best!

I like to describe myself as an "extra" extrovert. By that I mean there are people who are the stereotypical extrovert--loud, outgoing, people lovers. I am the equivalent of a few of those kinds of people. I am perfectly fine being the center of attention, and oftentimes I prefer it. There was a time in my marriage where we were with a bunch of people and, as usual, I had the entire group busting up laughing. Everyone was cracking up except for my husband. I caught a side glance of his completely stoic and obviously annoyed face, and he later told me, "I wish you wouldn't do that."

Without even trying, I stopped being "the funny girl." It was already an area of strong insecurity anyway, so it became easy to stuff my humor and try to be more serious. Except I was dying inside, because that's not who God created me to be. That's one area I'm so thankful He brought healing to, and He used a couple of people who barely knew me to do it.

One was Val, the mom of one of my friends I had met in college at a

14

prayer event. She was at a summer retreat with me a few years ago and, at one point during the weekend, she sat me down for a talk. We barely knew each other, and she only knew a small fraction of my story. She told me that God showed her that I have a gift of humor and joy and that He wants me to not hide it. I was simultaneously happy and frightened to hear that God actually gave me those gifts, and that He wanted to use them to bless other people!

Then another time I was at a bonfire with some new friends I had met in Wisconsin after a day of ministering with Stirred Up, and one of their friends, Josh, showed up. As we were enjoying the fresh air of a summer night in the middle of the woods and singing worship songs together around the crackling fire, Josh spoke up. He said that God was showing him that I have a gift of humor and joy and to not hide it.

2 Corinthians 13:1 says, "in the mouth of two or three witnesses shall everything be established." I finally began to say, "Yes, Lord," and unleash my gifts of joy and humor. I didn't need another person to validate what Val and Josh had said; I just needed to believe it. Now I love being the funny girl with the world's loudest laugh. I'm ok being the "extra" extrovert and center of attention again. I know God made me to be that girl and I love it!

One of my favorite Bible teachers and preachers, Priscilla Shirer[3], says to "Speak God's Word over yourself until you've changed your own mind.". There is transforming power in declaring God's Word over ourselves. His Word has the power to break and replace every lie we have believed or may be tempted to believe in the future. When we speak the truth over ourselves, it will renew and change our minds.

Here are some truths you can declare over yourself right now:

I am loved and wanted.

I am chosen.

I am not a mistake.

I am more than a conqueror.

God knit me together in my mother's womb--He created me!

---

[3] Shirer, P. (Date?) Article? Retrieved from https://www.goingbeyond.com

God has a plan and purpose for my life.

God thinks a lot about me.

God is my defender.

God is my refuge, my shelter, my hiding place.

God is for me, not against me.

God blesses me with peace.

God takes great delight in me.

His banner over me is love.

His plans for my life are good.

Hosanna Poetry has a beautiful spoken word called "I Have a New Name." You can find it on YouTube, Spotify, and probably other platforms. It is saturated with truth about who God says we are. I encourage you to look it up and listen to it. Then listen to it again. It is such a powerful message to help uproot any lies you may have believed about yourself or God. I was super blessed to see Hosanna perform last year at a women's conference, and I let her know how much it has ministered to me in my single season.

Someone else who really made a huge impact during my healing journey is Christine Caine, so I can't write this chapter and not tell you about her. She is an incredible ministry leader who truly loves Jesus Christ. I have been blessed to meet her and see her speak at women's conferences a few times. Her book "Unashamed" helped me so much, that I've recommended it to and bought it for more people than I can remember. She has other great books and a lot of great teachings online as well (I still listen to her often). Look her up if you haven't already!

Another great option, especially for emotional and mental healing, is counseling. Please don't disregard or discredit counseling because of the stigma that our self-sufficient society attaches to it. There is absolutely nothing to be ashamed of for seeking wise counsel. I really believe the world would be much better off if people would see good, godly counselors and implement the advice they're given.

At the end of my marriage, I met with an amazing Christian counselor (shout out to Janelle!) who really helped me process my situation and cast a hope-filled vision for my future. I still seek counsel from older, more mature women in the faith. Pastors or ministry leaders are also great counseling options. We should all have good mentors pouring into us in every season of life. If you desire counseling or mentoring, pray about it. God is really good at giving us wisdom and at making the best connections. He is more committed to our healing and growth than even we are, and sometimes He uses other people in the process.

If you have brokenness in your past, painful experiences that you had no control over or even ones that you did, or have suffered abuse of any kind (physical, mental, verbal, sexual), God is your Jehovah Rapha, your Healer. Please know that you did not deserve abuse and that God never wanted those things to happen to you. He wants to set you free from past pains and heal you so well that, when you tell your story, it feels like you're talking about someone else, like it feels for me sharing mine. He is the God who heals. He is the God who redeems and restores. He is *for* you. He loves you. He will never stop loving you. I pray that you let Him love you and heal the hurt.

Chapter Three

Dealing with Disappointment

Now hope does not disappoint, because the love of God has been poured out in our hearts by the Holy Spirit who was given to us —
Romans 5:5

I had a friend tell me one time that I am not someone who just makes lemonade out of the lemons that life throws at me, but I make lemon meringue pies. Her clever and creative words let me know that she saw me as an extremely optimistic person, which was a compliment I gladly accepted. Disappointment is something we all deal with, but not something we all deal with well. Sometimes disappointment can be as frivolous as shopping online, only to check out and realize your items are no longer available, or it can be as devastating as craving Chick-fil-A only to realize it's Sunday and they are closed. Sometimes God shows us the bigger picture and purpose behind what we see only as disappointments and setbacks; but even when He doesn't, we can trust His ways.

Whether you naturally see the glass half full, half empty, or are asking "what glass?", life can hit you hard and knock the breath right out of your lungs. There are times when situations are much more serious than online shopping and Chick-fil-A. Like painful years gone by without a positive pregnancy test or another hopeful turned to dead-end date night. The more it matters, the deeper the soul cry is when our hopes aren't producing our desired outcome. We wonder if it's just the timing of the Lord, or if we are doing something wrong and somehow messing things up.

One of the most important people in my life has always been my Grandma. I spent many summer nights and weekends with her growing up. We'd often sit with coins in our hands scratching off lottery tickets, go to classic car shows (she and grandpa always had a classic car), and frequent our favorite restaurant, Taco Bell, together. She taught me how to swallow a pill so that I could stop taking children's medicine and coaxed me into trying new foods that I refused to try with my own parents. I have so many wonderful and funny memories with her and am forever grateful that God allowed me to be her granddaughter.

When I was twenty-two, she had her third open heart surgery at the Cleveland Clinic. I was naive, and possibly in denial, of the seriousness of the surgery. I had never lost someone super close to me and just didn't see death as an option for her. I stayed home while Grandma had her surgery over four hours away, believing that nothing would, or possibly could, go awry. At two a.m. I received a phone call from my crying mom asking for me to please pray. The surgeon had just told my family that Grandma's weak and frail heart had disintegrated in their hands. Hearing this sent my own heart into deep anguish as I pleaded for her life, begging God to not take this woman that I loved so much.

Miraculously, the surgeons were able to reconstruct her heart and keep her alive. Despite that wonderful answer to prayer, my Grandma only lived for two months after that. The loss of her life here on Earth was a deep and devastating loss for me, but I want to do what my best friend Anna always tells people to do--come up higher and see what God sees about the situation.

***

My Grandma knew Jesus, and I know she is in Heaven--reason to praise.

I got to see my Grandma a few times after her surgery while she was in ICU, despite the distance--reason to praise.

I got to spend valuable time with my Grandpa while in Cleveland--reason to praise.

I had twenty-two years with a grandma who poured joy into my life and loved me deeply--reason to praise.

My beautiful grandma was a well of wisdom and a source of laughter, generosity, and selflessness. Even eleven years later, my heart still grieves the loss of her and the disappointment that she is no longer just a phone call away. Allowing God to show me the good things, even in my disappointment, helps bring joy to the pain. Plus it helps to remember that when our loved ones know Him, it's never "goodbye," it's just "cya later."

There will be times, moments or even days, when disappointment seems to be the loudest voice you hear. Trusting God and standing on His Word during those times is crucial to not adopting a defeated mindset. His thoughts and His ways really are so much higher than ours. I challenge you to be tenacious about silencing the voice of the enemy and not wallowing in the disappointments of life.

1 Thessalonians 5:18 says that it's God's will for us to give thanks in all circumstances. Being thankful in the good times is easy, but it's during the trying times that we need to remind ourselves to be thankful. Those are the times when it's not our natural response, but when we need a shift of focus the most. I saw a sign at Hobby Lobby one time that read, "There is always, always, always something to be thankful for." When we choose to find things to be grateful for and give thanks, and even write them down or speak them out, it lifts us out of the pits of our devastations. We have to remind ourselves that no matter what happens in our lives, God is always good, and He never steps down from His throne.

I love what my friend Priscilla told me one time: never let the enemy see any part of you other than the bottom of your foot! I figure that means he can't be much bigger than a shoe size 7.5! It's important that we realize Jesus defeated the enemy and has given us the victory He won on Calvary. Don't make the enemy bigger than he actually is. The Bible says, "We demolish arguments and every pretension that sets itself up against the knowledge of God, and we take captive every thought to make it obedient to Christ." (2 Corinthians 10:5)

Sometimes the biggest arguments and pretensions (claims) that the enemy will throw at us are masked in what we accept as our own thoughts. The quickest and easiest way to know the source of a thought is to line it up against the Word of God. Know that if you are a born-again believer, you have the mind of Christ. (1 Corinthians 2:16) God will never contradict His Word so, if what you hear is contrary to the Bible, it's not from Him. Arrest every lying thought that enters your mind and declare God's truth in its place.

Here are some examples of lies and truth:

***

Lie: I'll never be good enough or have enough.
Truth: I lack no good thing when I seek Him. Psalm 34:10

Lie: I can't do what God has called me to. It's too hard.
Truth: I can do all things through Christ who gives me strength. Philippians 4:13

Lie: I don't have what it takes to be a good parent, a good friend, to start a ministry or business.
Truth: He supplies all of my needs according to His riches in glory. Philippians 4:19

Lie: I have been dealt a short-hand in life.
Truth: He gives me everything I need for life and godliness. 2 Peter 1:3

Lie: I have messed up too many times for God to forgive me.
Truth: His mercies are new every morning. Lamentations 2:22

Take some time to ask the Lord if there are any lies you have believed about Him, yourself, or your life. Ask Him to reveal the truth that will override and replace those lies. I did this recently, and God revealed to me that I had believed a lie that He was a promise giver but not a promise keeper. Whoa! That realization shook me to my core. I chose to forfeit that lie and confess that He always keeps His word and "God is not man, that He should lie." (Numbers 23:19)

I want to remain in a posture of continually giving God access to my heart and asking Him to search me so that I am walking in complete truth. Don't let lies settle in your heart. Quickly combat them with truth. Resist the devil, and he WILL flee! (James 4:7) Focus on what God is doing and has done instead of where you feel or see lack in your life. Put on a garment of praise for the spirit of heaviness. Praise Him for who He is and watch that heaviness lift! Keep your words and confessions in line with His truth. The truth is in His voice. The truth is in His Word. What voice will you choose to listen to?

One summer during college, I went to some neighborhood garage sales with my family. If you love garage sales, you know those are the best kind because you can park and hit up a bunch of deals in a short amount of time. I hit the jackpot early on in the day when I found a giant free table loaded with stuff. Free tables are gambles because they are usually filled with junk that no one wants, but this one was different. It was filled with cute purses and nice clothes that were MY size, so I quickly started loading up my arms with free treasures. The lady that was running the sale quickly came up to me and said, "Ma'am, that stuff isn't free, the table is." I was so embarrassed! Disappointed, I quickly dropped the items back on the "free table" and hurried out of there.

One woman who experienced a much deeper level of disappointment than my unattained garage sale items is Hannah, whose story can be found in the Old Testament book of 1 Samuel. Back in that day, some men had multiple wives. It's important to know that just because something happened doesn't mean it was condoned by God. Her husband Elkanah had one other wife, Peninnah. Not having children in the culture of that day was embarrassing and shameful. Children were viewed as a blessing and not having any had several negative implications.

Peninnah had several children and Hannah remained barren. As if it wasn't enough watching Peninnah give birth to child after child while her own desires remained unmet, Peninnah made her miserable with taunting and teasing. Hannah wept and stopped eating because her heart longed so deeply for children. In response to her anguish and longing, Hannah prayed this beautiful prayer, (1 Samuel 1:1-11):

O Lord of hosts, if You will indeed look on the affliction of Your maidservant and remember me, and not forget Your maidservant, but will give Your maidservant a male child, then I will give him to the Lord all the days of his life, and no razor shall come upon his heard.

God heard and answered Hannah's prayer and she conceived a son, Samuel. In time, she was also blessed with five more children. Hannah turned to God, the only One who could change her disappointing circumstance. He turned her weeping into joy and satisfied the longing of her heart. In 1 and 2 Samuel, you can read more details about the life of Samuel, who became a great prophet of God and anointed David as King over Israel.

Hannah's story is such an encouragement and reminder that God cares and is always attentive to the cries of our heart. What we sometimes see as delay or disappointment could actually be a setup for God's best plan and purpose. In the midst of the frustrations in life, it's not always easy to see that.

While part of the events planning committee at my job, I would get to run random errands from time to time. After our Christmas party one year, I dropped off our tablecloths at the local dry cleaner and planned to pick them up after a few weeks. Since it wasn't urgent to get them back right away, a few months slipped by before I realized I hadn't received a call to pick them up.

Over the course of nearly eight months, I made several phone calls and stopped by the cleaner only to be told they weren't ready, they were lost, they were at another location, and to call and come back another time. Honestly, it was very annoying and didn't make sense until the day I *was* finally able to retrieve our cleaned tablecloths.

For what felt like the millionth time, I entered the small brick shop on the corner, dreading that I may hear again that they were lost or not ready. The gal at the counter made my day when she pulled out the tubs of tablecloths and put them on the counter. It felt like having the Publisher's Clearing House show up at my door! I finally could stop calling and stopping by! Since she was new to the job, she had to ask for help collecting my payment.

A clearly distraught woman came up to the counter from the back of the store to help her. Through tears, she taught her how to use the register and apologized for being so upset in front of me. After she helped us, she quickly returned to the back of the store. While my company credit card was processing, my heart ached for her. I had wanted to pray with her, but since she had left so quickly, I almost justified not doing it.

Once the gal handed me my receipt, I asked her if she could please go get the other woman so that I could pray with her. She came back up front and explained that she had just gotten a bad report over the phone from a doctor and was scared. I hugged her and assured her that God loved her and was with her and prayed for her healing.

When I got back in the company van with my tub of tablecloths, I realized why I had to wait so many months to get them. I needed to be there on that specific day for that woman who needed prayer and encouragement. It shifted the way I view delays and disappointments. It also filled me with a desire for greater awareness to see people that I pass on a daily basis that also need someone to tell them they are loved by Him.

Romans 8:28 is one of my favorite verses. It is a constant reminder and promise to us that God works all things together for the good of those who love Him. That includes the disappointing and hard times that, in the moment, usually don't allow us to see how God could bring anything good out of it. Even as followers of Jesus Christ, we are not exempt from traveling through times of disappointment while we are living our lives here on this Earth. The beauty of being His followers though, is that no matter how much disappointment our seasons may contain, He is always with us and He never leaves us. We are never alone. We can take those lemons life throws at us and make lemonade, or better yet lemon meringue pie!

***

Hidden Poem

When I feel overwhelmed and life is just too much
When my aching heart is heavy, Jesus You are enough

You are the rock I run to, my forever firm foundation
You're the Creator that I cling to without fear or hesitation

When I'm weary and heavy laden, You give the rest I need
When chaos is consuming, You are the perfect peace

You're the still inside the storm, the calm in the commotion
You're the Truth in times of trouble, You set miracles in motion

When life seems uncertain and I don't know what to do
You are the way of wisdom, my hope is in Your truth

When my focus is fixed on You, my soul stays satisfied
You're my healer, my protector, the shelter where I hide

You bear every burden and lift every load I carry
You break every chain, You give strength when I'm weary

Your Word will sustain me while You're making all things new
My life is hidden in You Jesus and my heart belongs to You

Chapter Four

He Withholds Nothing

No good thing will He withhold from those who walk uprightly.
—Psalm 84:11b

Lavish love. Love that is elaborate, costly, and unrestrained. The kind most of us desire but few are willing to give. That is the kind of love that describes God. 1 John 4:8 tells us that "God is love," and we can trust that all of His motives and actions are derived from the very character of who He is.

Agape is the Greek word used to describe God's love. It is known as the highest form of love that exists. It is unconditional and selfless. There are four scriptures that I think of immediately when I think of God's love.

Greater love has no one than this, than to lay down one's life for his friends. John 15:13

For God so loved the world that He gave His only begotten Son, that whoever believes in Him should not perish but have everlasting life. John 3:16

But God demonstrates His own love toward us, in that while we were still sinners, Christ died for us. Romans 5:8

See what great love the Father has lavished on us, that we should be called children of God! And that is what we are! 1 John 3:1 (NIV-partial)

The beauty of Agape love is that it is real and it never changes, because God never changes. God doesn't just talk about how He loves. He proved His love to us when He sent Jesus to die for our sins and restore the relationship between us and the Father. He didn't wait for us to do enough good things or to earn His love. He chose to freely give all of Himself regardless of our lack of merit. If that's all He ever did for us, His love would have been proven, yet He didn't stop there.

God doesn't promise to give us everything we want as if He were some sort of genie in a bottle. He does, however, promise to give us everything we need pertaining to life and godliness. (2 Peter 1:3) God has many names in the Bible that describe who He is, similar to how we can have many names. For instance, one person can have the titles of grandma, mom, wife, daughter, aunt, cousin, employee, friend, etc. Each title comes with a different role and responsibility. Learning the names of God gives us deeper insight into His character and who He is.

Two of God's names that we find in the Bible are "El Shaddai," which means "my supplier," and "Jehovah Jireh," which means "my provider.[4]" Philippians 4:19 backs up these names of God by telling us that He provides all of our needs. I love the lyrics of an old hymn called "Great Is Thy Faithfulness" that says, "All I have needed thy hand hath provided." There is nothing in this life that we will ever need that He is unable and unwilling to provide.

***

Therefore do not worry, saying, 'What shall we eat?' or 'What shall we drink?' or 'What shall we wear?' For after all these things the Gentiles seek. For your heavenly Father knows that you need all these things. But seek first the kingdom of God and His righteousness, and all these things shall be added to you. Matthew 6:31-33

God promises to take care of the things that we need and that our job is simply to seek His kingdom and His righteousness. My mind floods with many of the stories I have heard, and even many of my own, where this promise is fulfilled. One story in particular that comes to mind is the story of a missionary in the 1800s named George Mueller.

***

The children are dressed and ready for school. But there is no food for them to eat," the housemother of the orphanage informed George Mueller. George asked her to take the 300 children into the dining room and have them sit at the tables. He thanked God for the food

---

[4] Author Unknown. (Date Unknown). 60. The Compound Names of Jehovah: Jireh, Rapha, Nissi. Retrieved from https://bible.org/seriespage/60- compound-names-jehovah-jireh-rapha-nissi

and waited. George knew God would provide food for the children as he always did. Within minutes, a baker knocked on the door. "Mr. Mueller," he said, "last night I could not sleep. Somehow, I knew that you would need bread this morning. I got up and baked three batches for you. I will bring it in." Soon, there was another knock at the door. It was the milkman. His cart had broken down in front of the orphanage. The milk would spoil by the time the wheel was fixed. He asked George if he could use some free milk. George smiled as the milkman brought in ten large cans of milk. It was just enough for the 300 thirsty children.

This story is just one of countless throughout history that prove again and again that God is our source of provision in every way and in every season. I encourage you to take time often to contemplate all of the incredible ways God has provided for you and give Him thanks!

When I started a middle school youth ministry a few years ago, I knew I was called and commissioned to teach and inspire a passion for the Word of God. Not knowing if kids coming would have Bibles or not, one of my first prayers was for God to provide Bibles for the ministry. The next day I received a call from a brother in Christ, who I had never talked to on the phone and haven't since, letting me know that he had connections to get me Bibles for my youth group if I needed them. That was such an incredible, and quick, answer to prayer! The Bibles not only had great study notes throughout the pages, which were very helpful, but they were all identical. Kids loved racing to find the verses so they could be the first to shout out the page number as we read the Word of God together. It was a huge blessing to receive that box of Bibles.

I have had many other endeavors throughout the years where I felt called to step out or step up to lead something, either in my church or community. More times than not, I chose to say "yes" before I had what I needed to accomplish the task. Those needs could be finances, volunteers, food or various other material items. Without fail, God has always provided all that I've needed, and often above what I needed, to accomplish those things He put on my heart to do. God will always provide everything we need to complete the tasks He calls us to.

I truly believe that God holds nothing back from His children, just like the chapter theme verse in Psalms says. This is a promise I have had to tell myself over and over again. Sometimes multiple times a day. His Word is so good, and it has sustained me during the difficult times I've encountered during my single season.

What does it mean that He "withholds nothing good?" It means that we will always have what He deems as "good" in every season, but we may have to swallow the reality pill that not everything we deem as "good" actually is good. As much as I have deeply desired a relationship during my single season, I am so glad that God has withheld one from me. I needed this season to heal and grow without the distraction of a relationship. When He deems it as good for me to enter a relationship, I will. Because I trust Him as Lord over my life, even when I think I know best or have a better plan, I fall back on the truth that He is who He says He is, and He will do what He says He will do. There is rest and peace in that truth.

It's important that we read the verse in Psalms in its entirety because the promise does have a prerequisite. It says that He withholds no good thing from those who "walk uprightly."

What does it mean to walk uprightly? Upright by definition means honest, honorable, high-minded, moral, ethical, righteous, and just. We only have the ability to possess all of these characteristics through Christ and the help of the indwelling Holy Spirit. Psalm 16:2 (NIV) says it perfectly: "I say to the Lord, 'You are my Lord; apart from you I have no good thing.'" Romans 7 and 8 describe the wrestling we face between our flesh and spirit; the want and will to do good, and the reality that nothing we do in our flesh produces anything good. God's Spirit allows us to live in a way that pleases Him and produces good things.

Ecclesiastes 7:29 tells us that God created us upright, but we have sought out many schemes. It speaks the truth that we were created to be upright because we were created in God's image, and He is upright. The battle with the sin nature that we deal with in this world is echoed in the lyrics of a hymn penned by Robert Robinson in the 1700s called "Come Thou Fount of Every Blessing.[5]" He wrote, "Prone to wander, Lord, I feel it, Prone to leave the God I love." Without the help of the Holy Spirit, we really are prone to wander and seek out "many schemes" that are ungodly and not upright in nature.

The best place to find wisdom on walking uprightly (or anything

---

[5] Robinson, Robert. "Come Thou Fount." *Penned*, 1758.

for that matter) is the Bible. Here are some verses that talk about an upright person, including God's promises for them (I encourage you to look up more!):

Proverbs 2:7 — *He stores up sound wisdom for the upright.*

Proverbs 10:9— *He who walks with integrity (upright) walks securely.*

Proverbs 11:3— *The integrity of the upright will guide them.*

Proverbs 14:2— *He who walks in his uprightness fears* the Lord.*

Proverbs 15:21— *a man of understanding walks uprightly.*

Proverbs 16:17— *The highway of the upright is to depart from evil.*

Psalm 11:7— *For the Lord is righteous, He loves righteousness; His countenance beholds the upright.*

*Note: This reference to fear means reverence and awe, not terror and fright.

Being upright, holy, and set apart is not always a popular decision in a culture and society that often (not always) rages against the truth. It is a choice that can be met with much criticism, controversy, and even hatred. Proverbs 29:27 states, "He who is upright in the way is an abomination to the wicked." That means that there will be people who won't like you. As a recovered people pleaser, that's not an easy thing to hear or say, but it's reality.

All of His good promises and the privilege of knowing Him are worth every bit of backlash we could ever endure during this vapor-like lifetime. Even though mockery, ridicule, and hatred don't forge warm and fuzzy feelings, I encourage you to walk uprightly anyway-- even if it means you're walking alone sometimes. The second stanza of my all-time favorite hymn, "I Have Decided to Follow Jesus," says, "Though none go with me, still I will follow, no turning back, no turning back.[6]" That has been the heartbeat of my faith journey even before I ever heard this beautiful hymn. In moments when I have felt like I am walking the faith path alone, I have moved forward despite it. As I've moved forward, God has blessed my life with very rich, godly

---

[6] Singh, Sadhu Sundar. "I Have Decided to Follow Jesus." Unknown.

friendships that have enhanced my life more than I can find words in the English language to describe it. Friends that love me, hold me accountable, pray with and for me, make me laugh, and challenge me to keep running my faith race, as Paul talks about in 1 Corinthians 9.

We do not serve a God of disappointment. His promises are *yes* and *amen*. (2 Corinthians 1:20) We have to know what His promises are though, and we can only know those promises by reading the Word of God. (Have you figured out yet that I love the Bible?). Some sources say there are over 5,000 promises penned in Scripture. I would say they are definitely worth looking up!

One of my favorite promises in Scripture that I share with others, and remind myself of often, is Psalm 23:6. It says, "Goodness and mercy shall follow me all the days of my life." It's a promise that stands on the good days, and also on the days that I wish I could do over. Goodness in Greek means "uprightness of heart and life," and mercy means "kindness or good will towards the miserable and the afflicted, joined with a desire to help them." The way God feels about me, and the way He loves me, is constant every single day of my life; it never changes.

There was one very special woman recorded in the Gospel books who experienced the unrestrained forgiveness, freedom, and love of Jesus and, in return, she gave her all to Him. I love the account in Luke Chapter 7[7] because it gives the most details. (Hello! I'm a woman and I like details!). Jesus was invited to have a meal at the home of a Pharisee (a religious leader). Most of the religious people were more interested in finding fault with Jesus than actually hearing the truth of who He was (the Son of God) and what He had to say. After hearing Jesus was there, "a woman in the city who was a sinner" showed up uninvited. With her reputation, the religious people would never have welcomed her into their homes. Her actions spoke louder than the words she failed to speak; no words were needed. She brought an expensive alabaster box, or flask, of fragrant oil, and wept as she washed Jesus' feet with her tears, wiped them with her hair, kissed His feet, and anointed them with the fragrant oil.

---

[7] Abraham, L. (2015, December 25). Weekly Devotional: Fruit of the Spirit – Goodness. Retrieved from https://www.gcu.edu/blog/spiritual-life/weekly-devotionalfruit-spirit-goodness

An alabaster box of oil was customarily given to women when they reached the age to marry and then broken at the feet of the one who asked her hand in marriage. Some sources say the oil was worth over $50,000 in today's US currency. Those in attendance at the dinner missed the beauty of the woman's display of love, because their attention was drawn to two other things. The first was the woman's unworthiness. They could not believe that Jesus would allow her to touch him because of her blighted reputation and questioned the truth of His claims because He didn't push her away or reject her. The second was the high value of the oil and what it could have been sold for in the market. They voiced ideas for ways the money could have been used better than dumping it on Jesus' feet.

Jesus took the time to correct their way of thinking and teach some very valuable lessons. I encourage you to go read the account in its entirety. He equated her great display of love to the fact that she was forgiven of much. Even though there are no words recorded that the woman spoke, Jesus took time to acknowledge her and speak to her. He told her that her sins were forgiven, her faith saved her, and to go in peace. I believe this "sinful woman" knew that no man would ever love her as much as Jesus, so she gave what was likely her most valuable possession, and in return He withheld nothing and said she was forgiven.

One of my newest favorite songs (I have many) is "Pieces" by Bethel. Find it on your favorite music platform and listen to it. Here are some of the lyrics:

Your love's not passive

It's never disengaged

It's always present

It hangs on every word we say

Love keeps its promises

It keeps its word

It honors what's sacred

'Cause its vows are good

Your love's not broken

It's not insecure

Your love's not selfish

Your love is pure

Love covers a multitude of sins. (1 Peter 4:8) There is no sin that is too ugly, too dirty, or too dark for God to forgive. As believers, sharing our stories not only helps us overcome, but it also helps others realize that God can, and will, redeem and save anyone who is willing to call on Him. His love never has, and never will, relent. It stops at nothing to pursue and prove itself. It's passionate and fierce. If He withholds nothing, why do we?

Chapter Five

His Promise, His Timing

Don't worry. God is always on time. Trust Him. —unknown

But as for me, I trust in You, O Lord; I say, 'You are my God.' My times are in Your hand. —Psalm 31:14-15a

Throughout my single season, I have been lovingly reminded, practically on repeat like a broken record, that the right thing in the wrong time is the wrong thing. The beauty of seasons is that they each bring unique differences appropriate for their respective times of the year. Living in Michigan has made me extremely familiar and well aware of the distinctive joys and challenges of drastically different seasons.

Winter months are filled with cold days, less sun, and a lot of snow, at least where I hang my hat in the Midwest. While some outdoor activities occur, they are usually short-lived as our time is mostly spent inside in an effort to stay warm and avoid frostbite. Nothing is planted or gathered, and the nights last longer than any other time of the year. This is a time when what we have gleaned in prior seasons becomes our sustenance.

Spring is the time of the year when we experience fresh, new beginnings. Winter has passed, and the increasingly longer days are met more frequently with warmth and sunshine. Flowers and trees start to bud, and the promise of new life mesmerizes those who open their eyes to behold it. As nature around us delightfully details the many nods of newness, our hearts and minds are also captivated with hope in the unfolding of fresh beginnings. We spring clean our homes to rid them of unnecessary clutter, and also take inventory of our personal lives and what really matters most. Seeds are planted during this time of the year in expectation of what will grow in another season.

Summer sees the longest, warmest days and the shortest nights as life teems with endless possibilities. Family vacations, road trips, beach days, stargazing, bonfires, theme parks and pool parties are some of my many favorite summer activities. I also love the spectacular display of fireworks that can be seen on Independence Day, after baseball games, and at other events. I especially love watching the reflection of fireworks dancing across the ripples of the Lake Huron waters up north. Like the explosives inside a firework, my heart bursts with celebration, rejoicing, and thankfulness when I see the colorful beauty paint the night sky. We tend to smile more and worry less during the sultry summer months.

Fall's diversely colored foliage paints our view of the outdoors with vibrant and breathtaking beauty. Seeing nature transform seems to happen stealthily, as leaves change appearance and begin to spill on the earth floor. This is the time of year when harvest happens. Seeds planted in the springtime have germinated during the summer months and harvest time has come. What was planted is now able to be gathered and gleaned.

The joys and challenges we face in each natural season throughout a year can be likened to what we also face in our many spiritual seasons of life. Identifying the season we are in helps us prepare and respond appropriately. When we sometimes feel like nothing is happening, it can be almost instinctive to reverberate the question in Psalm 77:8: "Has His promise failed forevermore?". When this question weighs heavy on our heart, we can respond confidently the same way Joshua did: "You know in all your hearts and in all your souls that not one thing has failed of all the good things which the Lord your God spoke concerning you. All have come to pass for you; not one word of them has failed." (Joshua 23:14)

The sustenance we injest in the seemingly never-ending winter months is His Word and promises. This is a season that feels harsh and even unbearable at times. We cannot rely on our erroneous emotions or flighty feelings, because they will always keep our train of thinking on tracks of untruths. We have to read and speak the truth regardless of what we see or how we feel in times when it seems like the better option is to just give up.

Springtime awakens our heart to the potential of all that He has for us. The reality that God has really good promises and plans for us causes us to "sow seeds" of prayer and water them with our faith and belief. We have to be careful to not "dig up" what we plant in faith by being double-minded (James 1:8). Whatever promise you are believing has to line up with the Word and heart of God. The best four words to speak any time we pray are "Your will be done," just as Jesus taught the disciples to pray, and as He demonstrated in the Garden of Gethsemane.

Summer is when we start to see our promises break ground, and the faith seeds we planted in the spring begin to bud. Hope is high for all of God's good plans as we eagerly anticipate stepping into the fulfillment of His promises. We have to carefully and constantly weed our garden of promise from the devilish devices of doubt, unbelief, faulty thinking, and enemy lies.

Fall is the time of year we all look forward to because it's the time for harvesting or reaping the promises God has given us. It's the season we all naturally want to skip ahead to, but we have to remember and realize that we don't get to the time of harvest without the preparation that takes place in the seasons prior. Galatians 6:9 is a promise fulfilled in this season as we reap the harvest of blessings rewarded for not growing weary and not giving up. It's good to remind ourselves of this verse when we are tempted to call it quits before we hit the harvest.

I made a list once of every instance when God has ever failed me. I didn't use a drop of ink because there has never been a moment in my life that He has not been faithful. Faithful is who He is! There are not enough songs to sing or words to speak that could exhaust the truth that He is a forever faithful God.

I love the lyrics of a really popular Elevation Worship song, "Do It Again[8]":

Your promise still stands

Great is Your faithfulness, faithfulness

I'm still in Your hands

This is my confidence, You've never failed me yet

---

[8] Elevation Worship. "Do It Again." *There is a Cloud.* Elevation Church, 2017. MP3.

God has never failed to keep His promises and He never will. I encourage you to take time often, even right now, to reflect on the faithfulness He has shown you in the past and thank Him for it. Doing this helps remind our hearts that He never changes and will always be faithful.

"But, beloved, do not forget this one thing, that with the Lord one day is as a thousand years, and a thousand years as one day. The Lord is not slack concerning His promise, as some count slackness, but is longsuffering toward us not willing that any should perish but that all should come to repentance." (2 Peter 3:8-9)

We can safely trust that His timing always has our very best interest in mind. We serve a God that exists outside of time. Our finite minds have difficulty understanding that truth, because we are so hard-wired with schedules that exist within the patterns of a twenty-four-hour timeframe. We are bound by time, but God is not.

Our culture sets standards that are often the furthest thing from God's standards. That includes the mold of when we should meet, fall in love and get married, as if that is something we can just "make happen." We run to the vices of social media or online dating sites when we feel like that allotted time gap is closing in on us. I am not saying these aren't ways we could meet someone and fall in love, but it's dangerous when we are motivated by fear to rush down those avenues. If God tells you to, then go for it! I know several people who have done so and are happily married. The point is, don't get desperate and start searching because you're eager to find an off ramp on the highway of singlehood. Stay on the road until God paves the off ramp, and that may be longer, or shorter, than you have planned.

Robert Schuler (a late American pastor, speaker, and author) once said, "God's delays are not denials." God choosing to navigate me through a season of singleness hasn't caused me to miss out on anything! And the same is true for all of us. We can grumble and complain, or we can choose to find joy in the journey. I choose the latter option.

One warm summer evening a few years ago, I was relaxing in my backyard in my extremely comfortable recliner chair that I got on sale at Kohl's (I love that store!). I had my journal on my lap and a pen in my hand, like I do so often. My view of the magnificent western sky was painted with a gorgeous sunset. My heart was yearning to hear from God and seek Him for direction concerning my journey of single-ness. I hadn't been single long and already had an intense desire for it to end. I never planned to be single again, and I was eager to not be alone anymore. God met me right where I was that evening in my little freshly mowed backyard. God knows the way we feel, and He wants us to be real with Him. He is always a safe place to let our guards down. It's part of the beauty of having a relationship with our Creator. We are granted the privilege of being authentic and vulnerable without the repercussions of forfeiting that relationship. He is not like that. He doesn't leave or forsake us, and He never will! Even in our most diffi-cult, ugly-cry, defeated feeling moments, He is close. So that evening I shared the vulnerable places in my heart with Him; the places that were hidden from the world but never hidden from Him. I came before Him humbly with all of my brokenness, questions, desires, and frus-trations.

That evening in my backyard, He spoke so clearly and so tenderly to my hurting heart. My restless heart that was longing for a good man in my life, while simultaneously wondering if they even exist. My bro-ken heart was tired of failed relationships. My defeated heart was done trying to make something work that was out of His will. My yielded heart completely surrendered to whatever He wanted to do in it. And the words of promise that He spoke have been an anchor for me since. He told me, "I am going to give you a husband who loves you like Christ loves the church."

That is exactly the way God instructs husbands to love their wives in Ephesians 5, and I was beyond ready for a husband that had a serv-ant heart and possessed the characteristics of the most perfect man to ever walk the planet, Jesus. I knew that meant he would be patient, kind, and unselfish, among many other beautiful things (see 1 Corin-thians 13 for a complete list of what real love looks like).

He also made it known that the timing was not yet. That is the point where many of us, me included, want to throw a fit! (Feel free to im-agine me lying on the ground kicking and screaming. It didn't happen outwardly, but it definitely did inwardly!). Waiting goes against the grain, against our flesh that wants what it wants and wants it NOW. I felt like I was handed a beautiful, but untied, balloon (hearing the promise), then forced to completely let it go into the wind and watch it slowly return to a deflated state (hearing I had to wait).

Or maybe a better analogy is that the balloon I was holding felt like it was quickly popped by a million unsuspected thumbtack, and, trust me, there aren't many sounds I appreciate less than the sound of a popped balloon. Being told waiting is part of the process can easily cause us to forget we are fortunate enough to have a promise to begin with. I wanted to be able to turn around and see the man of God that would love me in such a beautiful way standing right behind me. That would have been my ideal scenario.

But God is too good to give us something prematurely because it could, and inevitably would, destroy us. And even more than that, we would forfeit the beauty of the prior season He wants to navigate us through. Even though it could easily be my first prayerless choice, I will never choose microwave faith. That is a faith paved with the shortest route and least amount of prayer and belief required. The road less travelled may be longer, but it's filled with much more beauty; scenery that can't be seen on the more beaten paths.

As much as I truly didn't want to wait, I chose to relent my will to His. I chose to trust His timing (as I am doing still), and wait for His absolute best in my life. I chose to forfeit the feelings of wanting everything to happen fast. I abandoned my anxious hunt to "find the one" and just trust that when the time is right, He will bring it all together for me. I chose to focus my attention and efforts on what He wants to do in and through me during this season of singleness. I surrendered to all He wanted to take away or add to my life, show me, teach me, and work out in my often too-hurried heart. Why? Because I trust Him at all times, even when it isn't easy. (Psalm 62:8)

Trust is a "firm belief in the reliability, truth, ability or strength of someone or something." When you've had trust compromised in past relationships, it's easy to question the sincerity of someone's heart. I pray that if that's you, God heals your heart so well that you are able to trust Him fully and also, when the time is right, to trust the person He has for you.

The promise He gave me to bless my life with a husband who will love me like Christ loves the church wasn't for immediate claim, but to settle my heart with hope and trust for what He deems as the right time. I didn't need to be anxious about trying to make something happen, although the temptation to do so has definitely presented many opportunities.

39

One evening after work, in a rush to get out the door, probably to one of my volleyball games, I grabbed a banana to hold me over until I got home. The bright yellow peel gave no indication that it was underripe. I quickly peeled the banana, took a big bite, and just as quickly spit it out. Then the Lord spoke to my heart that there are times in my life where on the outside I may think something looks like it's ripe and ready, but only He knows what is happening on the inside. Ouch. Point taken, Lord.

And He was absolutely right, as always. There are times when we see someone that appears to be everything we desire, but we are only seeing the surface level. We see the outward appearance, while God looks at the heart. (1 Samuel 16:7) We need discernment from God to see deeper pertaining to anyone who may catch our eye and looks like they have it altogether (whatever that means) on the outside. They could go to church, tithe every penny they make, give to the poor, feed the homeless, and maintain all sorts of other outward appearances, but have a heart that is a million miles away from God. We have to seek the Lord because He is the One who knows the heart of the individual and can tell us if their heart is bent towards a fleeting facade or towards the Father. I want someone whose heart is bent towards the Father and whose good works are coming from a place of relationship, not an attempt to try to earn God's love or gain approval of man. I want someone who operates out of love, not out of obligation or selfish motive.

Many people throughout Scripture and the course of history have received promises from God followed by seasons of waiting. The Israelites waited forty years to step foot in the land of promise God had given them as an inheritance. Abraham and Sarah waited twenty-five years for the promise of their child Isaac. David waited over twenty years from the time he was first anointed king to step into that royal position of leadership over Israel. I know many people that have waited for the promise of a spouse, children, ministry, and other things and seen the fulfillment of them come to pass over time. Thinking about these stories, and countless others, of those who have received a promise, waited, and seen it realized, reminds me that God always keeps His promises. It gives me hope that He will always do what He says He will do in my own life as well.

My encouragement to you, and to myself, is to trust His timing completely in all areas of life. Only speak His promises, and guard your speech against anything contrary to what He has spoken to you personally and what is written in the Word. Meditate on Scripture and think about the things He tells us in Philippians 4:8. **Keep the vision of the promise plain by writing it down and putting it in a place where you will see it and pray over it.** Remember that His goodness and mercy follow you all the days of your life, and that includes every day of every season, regardless of how you feel or what you see.

All of His promises have a purpose, and they exist within the seasons He has assigned them to. He is more concerned about accomplishing His will in our lives than about snapping His finger to make our every wish His command. We can trust that the desires of our yielded hearts will happen, but sometimes it's a process and sometimes that process takes time. "When the time is right, I the Lord, will make it happen." (Isaiah 60:22)

Therefore the Lord will wait, that He may be gracious to you;
And therefore He will be exalted, that He may have mercy on you.
For the Lord is a God of justice;
Blessed are all those who wait for Him. —Isaiah 30:18

For the vision is yet for an appointed time;
But at the end it will speak, and it will not lie.
Though it tarries, wait for it;
Because it will surely come,
It will not tarry. —Habakkuk 2:3

Chapter Six

Preparation Season

Eye has not seen, nor ear heard, nor have entered into the heart of man the things which God has prepared for those who love Him. — Isaiah 64:4/1 Corinthians 2:9

What God has prepared for your life is bigger and better than you could even imagine for yourself. I believe your best days are ahead of you. That doesn't mean you will never face pain or difficulty, none of us are exempt from that; but even the dark spots on the canvas of life help paint the beautiful picture that is being created. God uses all things for our good. It's paramount that we prepare for what we are praying for. Inviting God into the process of preparation yields the most outstanding outcomes.

Being idle is not an option. We have to prepare for the promise, and *prepare* is a verb. It is a process that demands action. We were not created to coast through life devoid of meaning and purpose. Each season is filled with distinct assignments. Sometimes those assignments involve other people, and sometimes those assignments are simply to allow God to work in our own heart and life.

In the Bible, our heart is often compared to soil. Jesus tells the "Parable of the Sower" in Matthew 13 to a huge crowd of people. He explains that the Word of God is like seeds and our hearts are like soil. There are four different "ground" conditions that our heart can be in, and that condition will determine what our heart will do with the Word of God that we receive.

The first type of ground is "along the path" or "by the wayside." The seed planted here does not take root because of lack of understanding. When someone hears God's Word and doesn't understand what is communicated, the enemy snatches it away. Proverbs 4:7 is the perfect antidote verse for avoiding this type of ground: "Wisdom is the principal thing; therefore, get wisdom. And in all your getting, get understanding." When we read God's Word or sit with someone's teaching, either in person or online, praying for understanding of the Word is crucial. We want to hear the Word, understand it, and apply it to our lives appropriately.

The second type of ground is "rocky." The seed planted here also does not take root due to a lack of depth. The word that is planted is uprooted as soon as belief in the Word results in trouble or persecution. Following Jesus is not always pretty and popular. Consider many of the first century followers, whose decision to follow Christ often ended in martyrdom. While that may be extreme for our culture, it's not unheard of in some parts of the world today. Most of us aren't even willing to endure mockery and criticism because we care more about our reputations than we do about standing up for truth, let alone face a gruesome death for our faith. Romans 1:16 is one of my favorite verses: "For I am not ashamed of the gospel of Christ, for it is the power of God to salvation for everyone who believes, for the Jew first and also for the Greek." People haven't always sung my praises for choosing to follow Jesus, but I have chosen to follow Him anyway. Being unashamed and resolving to live for God despite trouble and persecution keeps our heart from being "rocky."

The third type of ground is "among the thorns." Seed received to this kind of ground is choked out because of worldly cares and the deceitfulness of riches. The world tempts us with a lot of empty promises, trying to pull us onto the hamster wheel of vain pursuits. The problem with that wheel is that it never goes anywhere significant or worthwhile. It chases after things that don't matter. Nothing in this world will ever be worth more than a relationship with God; nothing even compares to it. I want my ambitions and the pursuits of my life to be eternally focused. Colossians 3:2 tells us to set our minds on things above, not on things of the earth. Is what we are doing day in and day out more focused on this temporary life and our own comforts, or do we focus on things above, knowing God, and making Him known to others?

The fourth and final type of ground described in the parable is the type that we should all want: "good ground." This is ground where seeds are planted and fruit is yielded in measures of hundredfold, sixtyfold, and thirtyfold. This is someone who hears the Word and understands it. When we know what the Word of God is saying and properly apply it to our lives, that is when we are most effective, and His Word does what it is intended to do--shape and mold our lives. Isaiah 40:8 says, "The grass withers, the flower fades, but the word of our God stands forever." Everything in this short life is so temporary, but His Word will live on for eternity. I want the seeds of God's Word to yield abundant fruit in my life.

I encourage you to take time often to contemplate and inspect the condition of your heart. Allow God to show you any areas that need to be cleaned or changed. Let the Holy Spirit act like an around-the-clock pool inspector when it comes to your heart. "The Pool Butler[9]" says:

***

In addition to the pool itself, a pool inspector will inspect all of the pool equipment. This includes filters, pumps, heaters, plumbing, timers, and any other electrical components involved in the pool's functioning. The goal of a professional inspector is to determine what damage, if any, is affecting the pool.

It doesn't matter what damage has been done to you, or even what damage you have done to yourself. You are the only one responsible for the condition of your own heart. If your heart is muddy and mucky, it's your responsibility to remedy it so that it's pure and clean. You don't have to continue living one more day with a bruised, battered, and damaged heart condition. Because ultimately, God has given you everything you need to assess and change the condition of your heart, through His love, His Word, and His Spirit. You just have to simply open your heart and let Him do it.

Preparation season is also a time to discover yourself. One of the best pieces of advice I have been given is that God doesn't unite two halves, He unites two whole people. I want my future marriage to complement my life, not complete it. Know that you can be completely whole as a single person. Expecting another person to complete us is an unfair pressure we should never put on someone. Take this time to figure out and pursue what you love. Realize more things about yourself. Look at this season as an opportunity to grow. Learn new things, see new places, and actually enjoy your life. It's the only life you will

---

[9] www.thepoolbutler.net

ever get.

I have learned that I *love* creating and checking things off a bucket list. My friend Rachy and I were having a girls' day at my house one weekend. She read an excerpt from a book that prompted us to each write a list of twenty-five bucket list items. The book encouraged us to write down everything, big or small, that we desired to do or accomplish. I thought the task sounded fun, but I was also reluctant because I didn't think I could even come up with ten things, let alone twenty-five I do love challenges, though, so I agreed to do it. With pen in hand and my journal wide open, I went to town writing every single bucket list item I could think of. Nothing was exempt from inclusion if it crossed my mind. And I was shocked when my list surpassed twenty-five and ended up being closer to fifty. Rachy's list was also super long. We probably could have kept going, but we decided to cut ourselves off.

I loved letting myself dream about and ponder the things that I actually desire to do and accomplish. I wrote down that I want to have a picture of a sunflower in my home. Sunflowers have become a special symbol of the Father's love to me. My friend Amy later helped me create and print a beautiful picture of a sunflower field with my favorite verse (Ephesians 3:20), which I framed and displayed on my fireplace mantle. I also wrote down that I want to visit all fifty states. When I became single, I had only visited six states. As of today, I have been to thirty-two. Traveling is a desire that I never even realized I had until I became single. God has blessed me with many opportunities to see so much more of the world beyond my small city limits.

A few summers ago, I took my first long road trip with my niece, Makayla. We left our familiar mitten state and traveled east in pursuit of new sites and new memories. We went to Niagara Falls, and the Hornblower cruise took us out very close to the falls, which was both overwhelming and breathtaking! Even with ponchos on, we were completely soaked. My heart was so full of joy, and I laughed a lot as the intense pressure of the falls rocked our boat. We visited a quaint place about a half hour north called Niagara-on-the-Lake. The shores of the town meet up with Lake Ontario, which was the last of the five Great Lakes I had yet to visit!

We then traveled across New York, Vermont, and New Hampshire to the coast of Maine and stayed at a place right on the waters of the

Atlantic Ocean. It was INCREDIBLE! Being able to see the sunrise over the ocean from the coast of Maine was a desire in my heart, and it was fulfilled. After that we drove through the smaller states on our way to New Jersey and took a ferry boat to New York City for a day. We ended our trip with a full day visiting friends in Pittsburgh before heading back home to Michigan. So many great things happened on that trip; more than I have space here to write about. We met the most interesting people, ate the best cheeseburgers in Massachusetts, and beheld some of America's most beautiful scenery.

I have also been blessed to visit caves in Kentucky, the mountains in Tennessee, Disney World, Mount Rushmore, the Badlands, Tahquamenon Falls, Pictured Rocks, Branson in Missouri, and so much more. I've been able to see places I never imagined I'd see--things I didn't even know existed. I've taken a few longer road trips, some flights to further places, and many more local day trips. I have definitely, without a shadow of a doubt, been bitten by the travel bug. Actually, I imagine that my entire body has been infected, because I am constantly daydreaming about my next adventure and place to visit. And to think most of my traveling didn't even begin until I was single!

Don't limit what God can do because of your own lack of ability, time, or even income. Financially speaking, it doesn't make sense that I should even be able to afford some of the experiences I've had, but somehow God has made a way. Don't wait to be in a relationship to live your life. Have fun, try new things, go after your dreams and accomplish your goals now. And if you know other singles, encourage them to do the same. If you're already in a relationship, don't stop setting goals and chasing your dreams. Be driven and ambitious in the pursuit of things God has for your life. Writing a book has been a dream of mine nearly my entire life, and it is something I didn't even attempt to do until I was single.

If you want to try a new career or go back to school then apply for new jobs or sign up for a class. Don't wait for someone to be by your side before you begin doing things that better yourself and your life. When you are single you have the most amount of time to do those things without distraction. Seize the opportunities God brings into your life and guard against selfish and nugatory pursuits. Invest yourself in things that matter and will contribute to a better future for yourself and your potential future marriage.

I have told my friend Barbie that I want (let's be real--I *need*) her to teach me how to cook so that my future husband will not have to eat cereal every night. Even though there are plenty of varieties of cereal to choose from, I want to be able to make more than Fruity Pebbles and Cornflakes. I have taken this time to learn new recipes and try new foods, which has actually been fun. It's a very practical way for me to prepare for marriage, but also to enhance my own skill set. All kidding aside, I am really just praying my husband loves to cook.

One thing I am much more passionate about than cooking is community outreach. About six months into my single season, I had an opportunity to bring an organization called Break the Grey to local schools, with the help of a lot of incredible people. They reach middle and high school students through school assembly programs with motivational speaking, music, and skits on topics like substance abuse, suicide, self-harming, relationships, and self-worth.

The impact the program had on my hometown was huge, and the opportunity opened for me to become a Field Manager for the organization. So, I applied, interviewed, and accepted the position. And that decision has eternally changed my life.

In my three years working with them, I was able to help impact thousands of students with strong and hope-filled messages. On a personal level, I gained some of the very best mentors and richest friendships. My personal skills increased in many areas, including public speaking, organizing, fundraising, and working with people. I also met my best friend, Anna, and we started our own ministry, Stirred Up Women, which is now where my focus and heart is. Sometimes God only has us as part of something for a short time, and the reason is much greater and grander than we realize in the beginning. Letting Him orchestrate my life has never left me unimpressed.

Other things that God has led me to do and accomplish during my single season are:

***

Starting and writing my own blog.

Having my own column in the local newspaper.

Being a part o and /starting different ministries.

Speaking at women's retreats.

Hosting women's prayer nights and small groups.

Starting a family Bible study.

Writing poetry (and sharing it once at an open mic night in Florida).

Starting my own podcast.

I share these things to encourage you to not waste your single season. What God has had me do may look absolutely nothing like anything He will ever have you do. My heart is for you to hear His voice and do only what He instructs *you* to do. Be brave enough, like Peter, to step out of your boat, even if no one else does. Sometimes when we do, it gives others confidence to do the same. Know that God will fully equip you and help you accomplish everything He calls you to do.

As a single, I have discovered so many things about myself. I have a love for fashion I never knew existed. If only my budget matched my level of love! I actually enjoy spending time in a fitting room trying on different ensembles and piecing together wardrobes. I love pairing jewelry and shoes with stylish outfits and creating cute looks. Someday I would love to have a giant walk-in closet!

I also have learned that I love coffee, which definitely makes my adulting game stronger. I enjoy it even better when I'm drinking it with a friend and having good conversation. Some of my favorite friendships began over a cup of coffee. It's very common for me to invite someone to a local coffee shop to get to know them. There is something about a coffee shop setting that makes me super happy.

Focusing on pouring into others has been one of my single-life ambitions. I love finding ways to be a blessing and take the focus off myself sometimes. One Valentine's Day, I hosted a get-together at my house for single ladies. I ministered to them with food, fellowship, and encouragement. We laughed, shared stories, prayed and listened to a powerful message by Hosanna Poetry.

Since I don't have my own children yet, I have stepped up my "aunt" role, both to my biological nieces and nephews, and the ones I've adopted into my life along the way. We have sleepovers and go on fun outings and also gives their parents a break (win/win).

I encourage you to get involved in things that matter. Impact your world. That could be ministry, tutoring, volunteering at a non-profit, visiting an elderly person at a nursing home, sending someone a text or calling them, dropping off flowers at someone's doorstep, or setting up a coffee date with someone. The possibilities are as endless as the stars in the sky.

Invest in the lives of others every chance you get, and also focus on growing in your faith. Colossians 2:6-7 (NIV) is my prayer for every reader: "So then, just as you received Christ Jesus as Lord, continue to live your lives in Him, rooted and built up in Him, strengthened in the faith as you were taught, and overflowing with thankfulness." Read, receive, and root His Word deep into your heart.

Learn to be thankful for and love the life you have been given. Not your best friend's life. Not your favorite celebrity's life. *Your* life. Pursue Your Passions.... PASSIONATELY. You may first have to take time to discover what you are even passionate about. And that's okay. Let this season serve to prepare you for what God has next for your life. Take time to learn every lesson, see every sight, hear every word He speaks, go everywhere He calls you to, and discover things you haven't yet. Don't get anxious about what's ahead and miss what is happening now. We only get one life, so make the most of every day you are given. A season of preparation is full of purpose, and I pray your heart is encouraged in knowing that what God is preparing for you is much greater than you can even imagine.

Chapter Seven

Wait Well

Wait on the Lord; be of good courage, and He shall strengthen your heart; wait, I say, on the Lord! —Psalm 27:1

Waiting should be anything but passive. How we spend any season of our lives is completely our choice, and I pray that you choose to walk intentionally through seasons of waiting, allowing God to work in your life while you anticipate whatever it is you are praying for. I believe every day we are given is a gift, whether we are in the wallows of waiting or walking in the fulfillment of our promises. A season of waiting bathed in prayer, communion with God, and serving others will take the focus off ourselves and help us make the most out of the time we are given. We can determine to wait on the Lord, knowing He promises to strengthen our hearts when we do.

One of my favorite songs that paints a picture of waiting well is "While I'm Waiting" by John Waller from the inspirational movie "Fireproof":

***

I will move ahead, bold and confident

Taking every step in obedience

While I'm waiting

I will serve You

While I'm waiting

I will worship

While I'm waiting

I will not faint

I'll be running the race

Even while I wait

We can confidently rely on and fully believe His promises while simultaneously experiencing the pangs of waiting. I have found that I get very weary when my focus is on the grains slowly slipping through the sand clock and, just when I think the time of waiting is up as the last grain falls to the bottom bulb, the timer is turned over and starts again. Not knowing how many times the clock will be flipped is exhausting and disheartening.

I have had to learn to trust the allotted amount of time God has set for my single season without fixing my focus on the "not moving fast enough" clock. The Bible says to have anxiety for nothing, and I have had major anxiety in wanting to know the details of the relationship God has for me. My anxiety came in the form of obsession, really magnifying my lack of trust in Him. Shifting my gaze to what God wants to do in my life in the meantime has been a significant source of freedom in my heart and mind. Waiting well includes looking forward to the promise with anticipation, but also actually living the season you are currently in with joy and enthusiasm.

When we go to restaurants and are told we have to wait, we are tempted to leave and go somewhere else, even though we'd be seated and ordering our food by the time we got back in our car and drove to another place to dine. We pay extra money to subscribe to television and music streams that allow us to skip commercials and eliminate any sort of wait between segments of shows or songs. Our human nature is wired to resist waiting and to constantly keep our thumb on the fast forward button of the imaginary remote control of life, even when it doesn't make sense.

The pause before the promise is not easy. Waiting for any length of time can quickly grow wearisome and frustrating. As I have faithfully prayed for my future husband over the past few years, God has repeatedly spoken two words to me--*wait* and *timing*. In a conversation with one of my good friends, I shared my heart regarding the future relationship God has for me. She told me that she felt like God was saying "it's not the right time yet." While I wanted to hear her say "get ready, it's going to happen tomorrow," or even later that day, would have worked for me, I am thankful that she boldly and honestly communicated the truth. We need to speak the truth in love to one another, even when it's not necessarily what we want to say or hear. Her words settled my heart and confirmed what God was already showing me.

God's promises are not like pudding or mashed potatoes--they are rarely instant. We will almost always choose the path of least resistance, the easiest and shortest way, and the route that requires the least amount of time, sacrifice, and cost. Those self-paved paths strive for immediate gratification while forfeiting the beautiful and important purposes God has for us on the path He has directed and designed for us to travel.

God promises to work all things together for our good, so don't rush to make something happen in your own strength and willpower. The option to circumvent waiting always presents itself, but not without costly ramifications. Consider how Abraham handled his "this is taking too long" promise. In order to fulfill the promise God gave him of becoming a father of many nations, Abraham took the advice of his wife Sarah and slept with her servant, Hagar, in order to have a child. While this was not an uncommon practice in that day as a means to gain descendants, it was not the plan God had for Abraham.

After approximately eleven years of waiting, Abraham and Sarah didn't believe God could possibly fulfill His promise of "descendants as numerous as the stars" through her elderly body that seemed to be out of commission, so they settled and devised their own plan. Despite the mess of initially doing things their own way, twenty-five years later God did fulfill His promise, in His perfect timing, through Sarah, just as He had planned to do all along. We see the beauty of God's promise fulfilled, but study further in Genesis to see the heartache and turmoil that Abraham's rushing caused him. Even in modern times, we can see the effects of pushing the promise in the continued conflict in the Middle East. The desire for the promise in and of itself was pure, but it turned into a disaster when they took matters into their own hands and tried to make it happen outside of God's will and way.

Instead of trying to force a promise to happen in ways we think will work, stay mindful to continually put and keep the promise in God's hands, and shift your focus back to what He has for you in the present.

Believe and pray for the promise, but don't let it become an idol in your heart and mind. One way we can identify that something has become an idol in our lives is when it consumes our thoughts and we become anxious about it. An article I found online pens it perfectly: "If you're looking to any relationship or material thing to give you what only God can give you, that thing is an idol in your life.[10]" That includes identity, security, love, rest and hope. It's important to constantly examine our heart to be sure we haven't erected any idols and repent if we have.

No human being can satisfy the longing in your heart that is only meant to be fulfilled by the One who created it. When you find your identity, purpose, and passion in Him, you will be content in singleness or in a relationship. Your soul sustenance and satisfaction aren't dependent upon your relationship status; it's based on your relationship with God. So, take time during this season to grow closer to Him.

One of the biggest blessings in my life has been the "spiritual mamas" God has given me, both in real life and those that I admire from a distance. I encourage you to pray for and find someone, or "someone's," who can pour wisdom into your life in every season. My spiritual mamas are women who are more seasoned in the faith, know and love the Word of God, and exemplify admirable character, and how I want to be as a Christian woman.

Charlotte Gambill is one of my favorite spiritual mamas. She and her husband Steve lead LIFE church in England, and she also writes and travels the globe lecturing. Her website bio[11] describes her perfectly: *Charlotte has an infectious love for life, a deep love for people and zealous love for God's House. Her passion is to build the local church across the earth, to see people reach their full potential and to develop and strengthen leadership. Charlotte is known for her practical, humorous and passionate application of God's word. Her messages of life and purpose are rallying a generation to embrace the broken and become ambassadors of hope.*

I have spent hours watching Charlotte's video teachings online. She is a powerhouse, an anointed woman who knows and loves the Word

---

[10] https://nickcady.org/2016/10/27/3-ways-to-identify-idols-in-your-life-what-to-doabout-them/

[11] Gambill, C. (Date?) Article? Retrieved from www.charlottegambill.com

of God. She has a gift of teaching the Bible in a way that is both under-standable and relatable. I had the privilege of meeting her a few years ago with Natalie Grant at a Dare To Be conference. What a blessing Charlotte has unknowingly been in my life!

One of her teachings is called "Doorways, Hallways, and Gateways" (you can find it on YouTube). At any point in life, we can find ourselves in one of these three places. Each position requires something differ-ent out of us--different focus, stance, and action. Her wisdom and ad-vice in navigating transition and waiting well is deep, and I encourage you to check out her videos and books.

While we are waiting for a door to open (relationship), we have to praise Him in the hallway (singlehood). Don't wait for "what's next" or "the next thing" to rejoice. There is value in every season, and you would be doing yourself a deep disservice overlooking or not believ-ing that truth. Praise God in the waiting, and don't forfeit one thing He has for your life.

The time you have as a single person, or in any season of waiting, is necessary, and how you spend it is crucial. Don't let the pages of your life pass you by as you try to force, close, or skip past the chapter you're in. I love how Kimberly Jones (another of my favorite lady preachers) puts it: "How you leave one season is how you will enter the next.[12]"

We are wonderfully created, but sometimes the world erodes us. If you are constantly complaining, unhappy, anxious, dissatisfied, and discontent as a single, you will be the same way in a relationship. Think about the person you want to be and, in reality, who you were created to be, and allow God to work in your heart and life and trans-form you more into His image. He has the power to change us from complainers to celebrators, unhappy to happy, anxious to carefree, dissatisfied to satisfied, and discontented to contented.

One prayer during this season that I have had is for God to cultivate a thankful heart within me. I want to have an attitude and outlook that not only honors Him, but also one that I enjoy being around. After all, I am stuck with myself every single day of my life. Let's be people who

---

[12] Jones, Kimberly. www.realtalkkim.com. www.facebook.com/realtalkkim.

rejoice always, pray continually, and always give thanks (1 Thessalonians), because Scripture says that is His will for us.

Waiting well looks like letting God work in us to prepare us for what He has promised. We can't be too prideful to think there is nothing in us that needs to possibly be pruned or changed. A few weeks ago, I was sitting outside reading a really good book about godly relationships (another great way to prepare). When I finished reading, I sat in my chair not ready to abandon the sunshine of the outdoors. I began praying for God to build my character and prune anything inside of me that needed it, while not actually thinking there was anything that needed to be dealt with. That's laughable, so feel free to chuckle before reading on.

He began showing me that I avoid expressing how I feel when it involves confrontation that could potentially hurt or upset someone. That's not a thrilling struggle to admit to, but it's real life. Not only that, but He showed me someone specific that I had been avoiding because I didn't want to have the difficult conversation that involved unresolved conflict. The beautiful thing about God revealing those "ugly" spots in us is that He always does it with grace and love and shows us how to mend the mess and fix the faults. He doesn't heap shame and embarrassment on us when He corrects us. Even though it's painful to be pruned, I welcome it in my life because I don't want anything holding me back from the very best life God has for me. I am determined that I will speak up and have hard conversations when necessary, and I know He will help me in doing so.

Intentional is a popular buzzword that I love. It means deliberate, planned, willful, and purposeful. Those are all words that I want to use to describe how I approach the season of singlehood, and every season of life I find myself in. I don't want to skip flippantly through my days void of purpose in a ho-hum fashion. I believe God has more for our lives than mediocrity. What that looks like for us individually will vary, but God will show you how to live intentionally with your own life.

One intentional thing I have done since I became single is to pray for my future husband. I have a specific spot on my way to work each day where I pray for him. I pray a lot of general prayers (for his health, his relationship with God, etc.), and I also pray a lot of specific prayers as God lays things on my heart to pray. There are other times God puts it on my heart to pray for my future husband, so I pray then as well. Praying for him is a privilege for me, and I encourage you to pray for your future spouse and keep praying for them after you're married.

Another fun and intentional thing I wanted to do while single was to write my future husband letters before our relationship starts. I tried finding the "perfect" journal to do this but couldn't find one that I liked, so I decided to write digital letters instead. I created an email account, and whenever it's on my heart, I send him a message. Sometimes they're serious and sometimes casual and light-hearted; whatever is on my heart and mind at the time. I share about what is going on in my life, the ways I am praying for him, and my pledge and commitment to wait well during this season without him. My plan is to give him the password when we get engaged.

I believe God is preparing the man He has for me, and that is something I am willing to be patient for. I also know that this is not just a time of God preparing him for me, but also a time of God preparing me for him. The Lord knew I needed to go through healing, grow in my faith, and figure out who God created me to be during this season of being single. I will forever be grateful that God didn't give me a relationship when I wanted it (right away).

I pray for God to mold me into the person my future husband desires and needs. I don't believe God wants or asks us to change who we are, but sometimes there are things we have allowed, knowingly or not, that were never God's best for us. There are ungodly mannerisms, habits, and behaviors that we would be wise to allow God to work on while we are single. Let God work in your life to make and mold you into the person you were always meant to be.

The best example we have to follow of someone who lived their life purposefully is Jesus Christ. The first account of His life that we read about in Scripture beyond His birth occurs when He was around twelve years old. Even at such a young age, He announced that His intent was to "be about the Father's business." (Luke 2:49) Jesus' entire life, which you can read about in the Gospel books (Matthew, Mark, Luke, and John) was completely committed to doing the will of the Father. He accomplished what He was sent to Earth to do--destroy the works of the devil. (1 John 3:8)

God has purposes and plans for your life that are much bigger than a relationship status. Instead of waiting idly and striving to fast forward through each day, we have to rise up and wait with wisdom and purposeful action. Focus on the assignments God has for your life and boldly accomplish them with the help of the Holy Spirit. Discover what you are passionate about and love doing and do it! If you don't know what those assignments are, ask Him to reveal them. I always tell people that two of God's assignments for all of us are to know and love Him and to love others.

One of my favorite pastimes is Christian concerts. I love Christian music and I love the atmosphere of being with a big group of believers worshipping God together through song. I found an organization about an hour from my hometown that puts on Christian concerts. For the first few years of my single season, I signed up to volunteer with them. I helped run merchandise tables, seat patrons, take tickets, and direct entrance lines. I made incredible new friends and met people that I'll probably never see again. It was a blessing to smile and speak life into whoever God put in front of me as I volunteered. I was also blessed at times with the opportunity to meet some of my favorite artists, like Jeremy Camp and Jordan Feliz, watch and worship at the concerts at no cost, and even be gifted with merch from artists when I worked at their table. As much as I desired to be a help through volunteering, doing what I loved actually helped me heal in more ways than I realized.

During my single season, God put it on my heart to start a middle school youth ministry called "Identity." For just over two years, I had the privilege of meeting with students weekly and teaching them the Word of God. We had snacks, played games, and simply shared life together. We did community outreaches, including singing Christmas carols at nursing homes and painting rocks with encouraging messages to hide around town. We also went on fun outings, like Yogi Bear campground, Michigan's Adventure, Sky Zone trampoline park, youth retreats and campouts, and ice cream nights. Whether I had two kids or twenty, my purpose and passion was to teach them about their true identity in Christ, dig into the Bible, and have fun while doing it. One thing I have learned after nearly fifteen years of being a Christian is that living for God is not boring. That's a blatant lie that I'll gladly spend all of my days eradicating.

I pray that you don't wait for a relationship to truly love and live your life to the fullest, because if you do, I fear you've already stopped living. I also pray that when you do enter a relationship, that you keep loving and living your life to the fullest. Discover and cultivate your passions. Find ways to grow in your faith and chase the call God has on your life relentlessly, without fear and hesitation. Look for ways to serve others and be a blessing. Don't idly waste your days away. Wait for God's timing for the relationship He has for you. And don't just wait, wait well.

Wait on the Lord; be of good courage, and He shall strengthen your heart; wait, I say, on the Lord! — Psalm 27:14

...those who wait on the Lord shall renew their strength...— Isaiah 40:31

The Lord is good to those who wait for Him, to the soul who seeks Him. — Lamentations 3:25

I waited patiently for the Lord; and He inclined to me, and heard my cry. — Psalm 40:1

Chapter Eight

Trust the Process

Trust in the Lord completely, and do not rely on your own opinions. With all your heart, rely on Him to guide you, and He will lead you in every decision you make. Become intimate with Him in whatever you do, and He will lead you wherever you go. —Proverbs 3:5-9 TPT

We can't lose sight of the promise because we can't see past the process — Allyson Rowe Schaffer

"God, You say to trust You with all of my heart, but what if all I have is a broken one?" This is a line from a poem I wrote during my single season as I longed to trust God but also felt the pull of impossibility in doing so. Trusting God with a fragmented heart feels like less than He deserves, but it's all that He asks us to do. Whether it's healed and whole or shattered in a million pieces, He is a safe place to put all of our trust.

Fully trusting the Lord can feel preposterous, especially if you have experienced broken trust in past relationships. The hurt and confusion that accompany broken trust with people we *can* see often causes us to question trusting a God we *can't* see. We project our experiences with human beings onto God and have a hard time trusting Him completely, especially regarding a promise of entering into a healthy and godly relationship.

One of the most freeing verses that I remind myself of often is Numbers 23:19. It says, "God is not a man that He should lie." We were created in His image, but He does not take on traits of broken humanity. Hebrews 6:18 reveals a powerful truth that not only does God not lie, but it's impossible for Him to do so. He can be trusted. Not a little bit. Not mostly. *Completely*.

I'm a word nerd, so let's look at some synonyms to really drive home the meaning of the word "completely."

Totally

Entirely

Wholly

Fully

Absolutely

Unreservedly

Every inch

All the way

Completely trusting Him means that we put our full confidence in who He is and what He speaks. We believe that He is who He says He is, He will do what He says He will do, and that His character is constant. If He makes a promise or speaks something, you can take it to the bank without even the slightest fear that the check will bounce or that the money is counterfeit. He will never fail in keeping His Word, both written and spoken.

So be bold and ask Him to speak promises to your heart. Start with cracking open His Word (the Bible) because it is a beautiful love letter that contains thousands of promises that are for YOU!

Write His promises.

Pray His promises.

Speak His promises.

Believe His promises.

I love to write scriptures and promises on index cards and tape them up on my bathroom mirror and on my refrigerator (two places I visit frequently!) to remind myself often of what I am believing for and what God has spoken to me. It's also a great way to memorize Scripture, which is very important to me. I journal Scripture and specific promises God has given me as well. Writing helps solidify information in our hearts and minds, so it's a tool I encourage you to put in your toolbox of life.

Praying God's promises is powerful. God doesn't forget His promises to us, but when we pray them it reminds our hearts of what He has spoken. It also validates that we trust Him to keep His Word to us, and it increases our faith for the fulfillment of the promise.

Speaking God's promises can look like saying them out loud to yourself as you go about your day or sharing them with trusted friends who will pray with and for you. Guarding my speech is something I take very seriously, so I try to be very intentional to not say anything that contradicts His written Word or what He has spoken to me personally, especially regarding a promise. For example, He has told me that He will give me a husband who will love me like Christ loves the church, so I will not say things like "I am going to be single forever" or "There are no good men left for me." God instructs us to not let any unwholesome talk proceed from our mouths, and to only speak what is useful for building us up. (Ephesians 4:29) I apply that Scripture to the way I speak to myself as well, because I want to build up my faith, not destroy it.

Believe God's promises, even when they seem outlandish and far-fetched. In 2018, God showed me that I was supposed to coordinate an outreach event at an area school. Many people voiced the impossibility of the situation, mainly due to the fact that the school is very influenced by the Muslim community. I chose to believe that God was going to pull it off somehow, even though I didn't have the exact details. God brought many people into the picture and, with the right connections, on March 7th the outreach happened. If God shows you something He has for your life, believe Him, regardless if anyone jumps on board with you or not. Our job is never to appease or follow the opinions of people, it's to live for God and believe what He says.

We cannot lean on our own understanding because it's too easily slanted by our experiences and emotions, which are often tainted by the corruption of the world. That's why renewing our mind is so crucial. (Romans 12:2) It's the only way we can truly be transformed to look less like the world and more like Christ. The word "renew" in its original context in Romans is a present progressive word. That means it is something we do now and continue to do in the future. Renewing our minds doesn't just happen one time, it happens over the course of our entire lives. We continually renew our minds by reading the Word and spending time in His presence.

One of my favorite desserts is Amish cinnamon bread. Several years ago, ladies at my church were on a kick with making it. Someone would give you a starter bag, which was a gallon size Ziploc bag filled with a sloppy wet mixture. For ten days, you had to follow the specific instructions to knead the mixture, add milk, and let the air out. Following each day's specific instructions was important because not every day was the same. After ten days, you were able to add the final ingredients and bake your bread. The satisfaction of smelling the bread baking in your home. then sinking your teeth into a luscious slice. made the tedious daily work worth it.

Single life, and life in general, is like the process of preparing Amish bread in many ways. We have to allow God to instruct us on a daily basis and do the things He tells us to do. He wants to guide our lives, but we have to let Him. Some days may look strikingly similar, other days may be as contrasting as the colors of the rainbow. Each and every day we are given has purpose. Following through with what God shows us may feel like work some days, but the good things it produces are worth every effort.

Whether you're loving single life, or waking up daily praying for it to end, these are days you will never get back. That's a sobering thought. I don't want to take any moment of my life for granted, single or not. I want to be like the Psalmist and rejoice in every day that He creates and allows me to live in. I encourage you to have a jubilating heart and be intentional to discover ways to praise and things to thank Him for. It'll keep your perspective upward and positive, I promise!

With all your heart, rely on Him to guide you, and He will lead you in every decision you make. Another version of this verse says to acknowledge Him in all of our ways. That means we need to include God in our lives, in our decisions, in our daily pursuits, in our dreams and plans. When we are at a crossroad and searching for direction in life, Scripture acts as the perfect compass. He wants to be a part of every aspect of our lives, and we would be wise to let Him in. He has something to say about all of it. Even the things you don't think He cares about, He does.

When I graduated college, it was on my heart to work for Oaklawn Hospital. I had heard so many great things about them, and their outstanding reputation definitely impressed me. I had never been a patient or even visited someone there, so I felt strongly that it was God directing me there. God speaks to us in different ways. Sometimes it's through impressions on our hearts that won't go away, which is exactly what happened to me.

As God would have it, as soon as I graduated college the perfect position opened up for me at Oaklawn. It was the right fit for my combined prior experience and degree. I applied, interviewed, and got the job. Working there for a few years not only gave me invaluable work experience to add to my résumé, but it paved the way for my next job. My time at the hospital also blessed me with great friendships and memories that still make me smile.

Like the time I bought fake lottery tickets from K-mart's gag gift section for my own birthday. My close friend and coworker Mae convinced our boss to join her in playing a trick on me by giving me the fake tickets in a birthday card. Little did she know the trick was actually on her. I played the part well, too! I casually scratched my tickets while my boss snickered behind me, actually believing she was finally pulling a prank on the renowned office prankster. I had tears running down my face as I enthusiastically declared my winnings that went from $5,000 to $10,000 to $20,000. My boss finally felt really bad about the prank and told me that the tickets were fake. I kept the joke going and pretended to not believe her. When I finally gave in to the fact that they were fake, I pretended to be extremely disappointed. Mae and I never did tell her that the prank was actually on her.

There was also the time I created and printed my own phony coupons for the hospital's coffee shop. I tried to use a "good for one free coffee" coupon, which they laughed at and wouldn't take. Then I tried to use a "BOGO Free" coupon, and that didn't work either. I paid for my coffee that day, but the laughs were worth my attempt at getting it for free.

The last funny memory that I'll share from my time working at the hospital was when I agreed to dye Mae's hair after work. I cannot confirm this, but I'm pretty sure that I let her know I had never successfully dyed hair before. Whether I did or not, I was clearly not a beautician, but that didn't seem to stop her from letting me take it on. She wanted a pretty blue chunk on the underside of her hair. I followed all of the instructions on the box and it looked really good...for a day. Monday, she came to work with a giant patch of orange hair on the side of her head. I blame cheap hair dye, not my lack of skill.

The desire and direction God put on my heart to work at the hospital produced not only a stepping stone on my career path, but it also gave me great memories. The process to get the job required action. I looked on their website for open positions, found the one I qualified for, applied for it, set it up and went to the interview, and accepted the job. I didn't go from thinking about a career at Oaklawn to the job without a process in between.

When we give the Lord complete access, it allows Him to place seeds of desire in the soil of our hearts. When we discover desires in our heart, we can first seek Him for clarity on whether or not that desire is even from Him. I want His desires to be my desires, because then I know I am in line with His perfect will for my life, but I am also not ignorant to the fact that not every idea or desire that I have is His. After we receive clarity, we can seek Him for direction on bringing the desires that *are* from Him to pass and ask Him to change any desires that aren't. He has a perfect process that leads us from a desire to fulfillment of it, and we can trust Him to order every step we take along the way.

A few years ago, I had an intense desire to sell my house and move to Texas to work for a ministry that dealt with troubled youth. It sounded like a good plan, but after praying I realized it was not God's plan. More recently, I had an opportunity to move to Vermont for a short time and stay for free at a beautiful bed and breakfast nestled in the mountains and focus on writing. It sounded like a dream come true to me, but through prayer I received a "no." We have to be okay hearing "no," and trust that there is always a reason when God gives us a red light, even if we never understand or figure out what that is. I never want to be confused by, or settle for, what's good over what's best.

How do we ready our heart to receive His desires? There are a lot of scriptures regarding the heart. Here are a few of my favorites:

Psalms 51:10— *Create a new, clean heart within me. Fill me with pure thoughts and holy desires, ready to please you.*

Colossians 3:15— *Let your heart be always guided by the peace of the Anointed One, who called you to peace as part of his only body. And always be thankful.*

Proverbs 4:23— *So above all, guard the affections of your heart, for they affect all that you are. Pay attention to the welfare of your innermost being, for from there flows the wellspring of life.*

Psalms 139:23— *God, I invite your searching gaze into my heart. Examine me through and through; find out everything that may be hidden within me. Put me to the test and sift through my anxious cares.*

The last part of the scripture says to become intimate with Him in whatever you do, and He will lead you wherever you go.

Let me say it again for the people in the back. He WILL direct your path. That word "will" is definitive and it's a promise. Not a suggestion or a close your eyes, cross your fingers and hope that it's true. It *is* true because the Word of God says it.

Psalm 37:23 says that "the steps of a good man are ordered by the Lord." I have seen Him direct my steps over and over again since I surrendered my life to Him over fourteen years ago. From jobs to ministry and everything in between, He has been the voice behind me saying "this is the way, walk in it." (Isaiah 30:21)

Become intimate with Him. Intimacy requires vulnerability. Be closely acquainted and familiar with Your Creator. Do you really know God? Don't settle for just knowing *about* God, because that is less than what He desires. Are you pursuing and cultivating a relationship with Him? He is intimately acquainted with all of your ways. (Psalm 139:3) Are you intimately acquainted with His?

His Word is a lamp for our feet and a light for our path. (Psalm 119:105) It shows us where we are standing and where we are heading.

If you get nothing else from this book, get this line: read the Word of God!

One more time: read your Bible!

I say that with a loving urgency, because I know so many people neglect the privilege of reading the Word. It is vital to your faith walk. Your life will never be fully satisfied as a believer if you are not reading it. Even if you hate reading, you can saturate your life with the Word of God by listening to it on audio. YouVersion is a free app that allows you to read and listen to the Bible with a few simple pushes of a button. It's super easy and convenient and completely eradicates the excuse of not liking to read.

I love reading my physical Bible, but I still listen to it on audio at times when reading isn't plausible (i.e., while I'm doing my hair in the morning, driving to work, or even while I'm sleeping). You can never hear enough of the Word of God throughout your day. In fact, the Bible even says that faith comes by hearing, and hearing by the Word of God. (Romans 10:17) Your faith is built by hearing the scriptures.

Knowing the Word of God helps you to understand the true character and nature of God. The answers to every question we could ask are all found in His Word and its accessibility, especially in the USA, which leaves us with no excuse to not know what it says. It's important to consume the Word daily for ourselves and not rely on others to spoon feed it to us on occasion. Spoon feeding leaves us malnourished and starved, and also at risk for false teaching and deception. If we don't know the Word for ourselves, we can potentially be led astray.

Spend time intentionally in prayer. Learning to hear His voice is vital because the world is full of mimicking voices and the enemy tries his best to throw us off course. He doesn't do that by coming at us with downright obvious opposition to God, but by making his voice sound as close to God's voice as he possibly can. The enemy wants us to settle for second best or "good enough," or as Michael Todd, pastor of Transformation Church, says, he wants us to settle for the "replica." But I refuse to have counterfeit Christianity and imposter plans for my life. I want all that God has for me, and nothing less.

John 10:5 says, "But they will never follow a stranger; in fact, they will run away from him because they do not recognize the stranger's voice." John 10:27 says, "My sheep hear my voice, and I know them, and they follow me." The Bible refers to Jesus as the Great Shepherd. Shepherds know their flock well because of the countless time spent with them. Sheep are with their shepherd so much that they will not answer to an imposter shepherd. We have to spend time with God and train our spiritual ears to distinguish His voice so that we will only answer to and follow Him.

Another cool fact about good shepherds is that they learn to call each sheep individually in a unique way. Each sheep responds to their personal call from their shepherd. God is that intimate with us, too. He speaks to us in unique, personal ways.

I was the leader of a recent women's event, and I asked the women to share ways that God speaks to them personally. The answers were extraordinary and unique, and reminded me that God does not speak to all of us in the same ways. It also encouraged us to look for the various ways God might speak to us other than what we might be accustomed to, especially when we feel like we are in a rut. God might speak to us through sunsets on Lake Michigan, through nature, and during prostrated prayer time. How God communicates to you may not be similar to how he speaks to those around you, and it could change throughout different seasons of life. The important thing is that you hear from Him, regardless of what that looks like.

Prayer is time we spend with God conversing. It's not just us coming to Him occasionally or flippantly with our list of needs. It's our time to, yes, bring our requests before Him--He wants us to do that; but it's also our time to hear from Him. To "get our marching orders," as my good friend Cindy says. He is not a silent God. He has things to say to us, so take the time to listen to Him speak.

We all approach prayer differently, and it can even change depending on the day. Some people thrive spending time with God out in nature, some prefer to shut themselves in their bedroom closet. We can pray throughout our day, and also set aside undistracted time to spend with God. He doesn't have limited office hours, and His ears are always attentive to our prayers. Regardless of what your prayer time looks like, the result should be the same: seeking Him with all of your heart and letting the dialogue be two-sided.

I want to give you some reminders and key points to discern if God is speaking. God always stamps His plans with peace. He is not the author of confusion or turmoil. You can know the character of God by referring to what is affectionately known as the "love chapter" in the Bible. (1 Corinthians 13) These are descriptions of what love is, and what it isn't. This is valuable to note because we know that God is love, and He will always operate and speak with love.

Love is patient, love is kind. It does not envy, it does not boast, it is

67

not proud. It does not dishonor others, it is not self-seeking, it is not eas-ily angered, it keeps no record of wrongs. Love does not delight in evil but rejoices with the truth. It always protects, always trusts, always hopes, always perseveres. Love never fails.

When you feel like He is speaking to you, ask yourself a few questions.

Does it line up with the character of God?

Does it line up with scripture?

If the answer to either of those questions is "no," then you can trust it's not God speaking. Ask Him to give you discernment and truth in the situation. Don't give up in the pursuit of seeking Him. He wants to be intimate with you as you trust Him and look to Him as your perfect Shepherd and guide.

I will instruct you and teach you in the way you should go; I will coun-sel you with my loving eye on you. —Psalm 32:8

There is a quote that says, "Jesus is my co-pilot." My pastor once said, "Don't let Jesus be your co-pilot. Let Him be the pilot and get in the backseat and let Him drive." I think that's so funny and really a better depiction of what God's role in our lives should be. While my driving record is near perfect, I tend to drive distracted and pay more attention to the music playing and hitting the right notes rather than focusing on my surroundings like I should. He, however, is the perfect navigator, dream director, and life leader. His focus doesn't shift, and His driving is always attentive. He is much better at getting me where I need to go, and He doesn't even need a GPS. I just need to trust Him and let Him take the wheel, like Carrie Underwood sings in her hit song, "Jesus Take the Wheel."

When you let Him lead your life, you can be confident that you are going in the right direction. His pace isn't hasty, and he doesn't rush, push, or hurry. He is definitely a God of epiphanies and break-throughs, but nothing He does is frazzled, scurried, or out of order.

You will be stretched. You will be challenged. You will be taken out of your comfort zone. Discomfort accompanies growth in the natural and physical world, so why would we expect to grow spiritually with-out some "spiritual growth pains."

One way in which God has really stretched me during my single season is to share my gift of poetry. I love writing and have enjoyed it pretty much since I could hold a pencil in my hand. For the most part, my writing hasn't been displayed for the public eye. Now I am not saying I am going to publish my journal pages. I would have to live underground if I did that because this girl gets super personal in her journals, and I am not looking for public humiliation! But God has had me start sharing my poetry. As awkward and uncomfortable as it can be to share your heart and soul in front of others, I still do it. One, because I desire to be obedient to Him. Two, because I have seen the ways my gift has encouraged, blessed, challenged, and ministered to others. And those two reasons alone are worth sharing and speaking up.

During a time of seeking the Lord intensely for direction a few years ago, He called me to a new church and to start a new ministry. Neither of those were even a blip on my radar. My plan was to stay at my church until they bury me in the ground. I am a committed person, and I loved my church (still do). I had absolutely no intention of ever leaving. Much like Ruth, when God said "go" and leave behind what was familiar, comfortable, and known. So, I did.

As difficult and challenging as that step of obedience was, it has been marked with incredible opportunities and blessings. I have been able to pour into the lives of teenagers that I would have never met otherwise. I've gotten to meet so many new people, which makes my extrovert heart explode with happiness. I have had the privilege to speak at my church a few times, cultivating a love for public speaking, which is something I never thought I would enjoy doing.

Each time I say "yes" to what God is asking me to do, He is growing my character, my courage, and my ability to see beyond myself. The Bible tells us to "do nothing out of selfish ambition." (Philippians 2:3) I want to live my life surrendered and truly let Jesus be Lord of my life. Lord means "someone or something having power, authority, or influence." I want Him to be the One who calls the shots. His plans for me and YOU are good!

Let Him pluck you out of your comfort zone; not much greatness resides there anyway!

Don't put God in a box and live in a box that is man-made. He is not a God who can be contained or completely figured out. Kick down those walls and step onto the path God has planned for your life.

Our life is like a puzzle, and we can only see the pieces that we have lived so far. God has access to the cover of the box. And what's on the cover? The big picture of what the beautiful puzzle of our life will look like. He sees the completed masterpiece, and He holds every piece of the puzzle. Don't try to create a picture of what your life will look like based on the limited pieces you have seen so far. I believe what God has for your life is exceedingly, abundantly above all that you could ask, think, or imagine. (Ephesians 3:20) Trust the process God has for putting the pieces of the puzzle of your life together, and let Him do it in His way, which is the very best way.

Our vision is restricted and near-sided, or better yet blind, compared to God's. Our minds are also finite, but His isn't. He knows the end from the beginning, and He possesses the fullness of understanding regarding everything. Ask God for His perspective on any season you find yourself in now or in the future. Don't get caught up comparing your life to anyone else's life, and let Him unfold the unique plan He has for your own life. The space between where you are now and where God is taking you has purpose, and He wants to do a work in whatever season you currently find yourself in. So let Him and trust the process.

Chapter Nine

Create Community

A man who isolates himself seeks his own desire; He rages against all wise judgment —Proverbs 18:1

Let us consider how to stir up one another to love and good works. — Hebrews 10:14

Isolation is an antique trick of the enemy. It's nothing newly devised or cleverly crafted. Proverbs describes isolation as selfish, and repeatedly in the New Testament, and specifically in Philippians, we are admonished to "do nothing out of selfish ambition." Without even realizing it, isolation can become a natural self-defense mechanism against potentially being hurt or the involuted vulnerability of letting anyone see who we really are. The ugly reality is that while we put up walls to keep others out, we inadvertently become prisoners within our own walls and keep the good things God has from getting in as well.

Having a good, strong community starts with allowing the proverbial walls to come down. That doesn't mean we have to open a giant gate in our life and let anyone and everyone in, but we should all have some healthy people with whom we can share our life. People who will love us well, speak truth, challenge, and stretch us. People who will stir us up and encourage us to be the person God created us to be. People who aren't afraid to call us out (in love) and call us up (higher).

I love knowing Jesus had a massive community (the multitudes), His twelve disciples, and His three inner-circle people (Peter, James, and John). All three groups were important, but not all of them had the same role, influence, and access to Jesus.

Community (according to Webster):

***

1. A group of people living in the same place or having a particular characteristic in common.

2. A feeling of fellowship with others, as a result of sharing common attitudes, interests, and goals.

The Bible has a lot to say about unity in the body of Christ. There is power against the kingdom of darkness when God's people come together in unity and operate from a united place. That is not just within a specific church family, but the church nationally and globally as well. The enemy thrives in the realm of division--within the church, marriages, families, and communities. Many scriptures encourage unity and warn against the perils of division.

1 Corinthians 1:10: *Now I plead with you, brethren, by the name of our Lord Jesus Christ, that you all speak the same thing, and that there be no divisions among you, but that you be perfectly joined together in the same mind and in the same judgment.*

Philippians 2:1-2: *Therefore, if there is any consolation in Christ, if any comfort of love, if any fellowship of the Spirit, if any affection and mercy, fulfill my joy by being like-minded, having the same love, being of one accord, of one mind.*

Luke 11:17: *But He, knowing their thoughts, said to them: "Every kingdom divided against itself is brought to desolation, and a house divided against a house fall.*

Romans 16:17-18: *Now I urge you, brethren, note those who cause divisions and offenses, contrary to the doctrine which you learned, and avoid them. For those who are such do not serve our Lord Jesus Christ, but their own belly, and by smooth words and flattering speech deceive the hearts of the simple.*

Knowing what the Word says about unity and division strengthens us to act in ways that promote unity and sharpens our minds to be keen to the devices the enemy uses to sow discord. Existing within a community that thrives on unity and will not tolerate disunity advances and glorifies God's Kingdom and dismantles weapons the enemy attempts to use to destroy us.

We know that from the beginning of human history, God created community. He made all of creation (the heavens and earth, the sun and moon, the animals--read Genesis Chapter 1, it's fascinating), and He declared that it was good. He saw the beauty of His wonderful creation and was satisfied with what His eyes beheld.

I recently went to the Creation Museum in Kentucky, which I highly recommend that you visit if you are able to. I watched a 4D show that marvelously portrayed the story of creation. It was so fascinating and extraordinary to see on a giant screen, especially with all of the 4D sights, sounds, and special effects. There were moments it was even a bit overwhelming for me to watch, so I can only imagine what it would have been like to actually be there and witness!

In Genesis 2, we read that after He created all other things, on the sixth day of creation, God created the first man named Adam. For the first time, He declared that something *wasn't* good, that man should not be alone. God's solution to the problem was creating Eve, man's first example of human companionship. We were not created or meant to live life alone.

Community is not just a *good* idea, it's *God's* idea. The beautiful thing about true and authentic Christian community is that it doesn't matter your age, what you look like, how much money you have, or what kind of background you come from. We are all connected through one common thing, the most important thing, and that is Christ.

I don't just want community. I want real, authentic community. Authentic community only happens when we all show up authentically, being exactly who God created us to be. We have to be brave enough to take off the masks and facades and just be real with each other. The body of Christ has suffered too much and for too long under fear and phoniness. People are craving *real*. Real conversations, real personalities, real people doing real life together. We spend way too much time and energy being jealous and critical, and comparing ourselves to one another. We do these things out of immaturity and sometimes even our own insecurities. Realize that God doesn't make mistakes, and we are all fearfully and wonderfully made. We are all image-bearers, and when we criticize one another, we criticize His creation.

I was at a women's conference one time and during worship the

Lord gave me this phrase: *break the measuring stick.* The only thing we should measure ourselves up against is the Word of God. When we measure against one another, we will always either justify and puff ourselves up at the expense of looking down on someone else, or we will feel less than, belittled, and not good enough. Both are dangerous traps.

2 Corinthians 10:12b:(NIV) — *When they measure themselves by themselves and compare themselves with themselves, they are not wise.*

(NLT)— *But they are only comparing themselves with each other, using themselves as the standard of measurement. How ignorant!*

Paul is talking to Christians here! We were not created for competition, so we need to stop competing with one another. I want to be the loudest voice in the ear of my brother and sister in Christ, cheering them on and encouraging them in their faith walk. I have no need to outrun or outdo anyone. I want to stay faithful in the lane God has called me to and champion others in their lane. We can't be each other's biggest cheerleader, though, if we are unwilling to be in community with each other. Proverbs 2:7 says, "He has stored up sound judgment for the righteous." Isolation goes against wise judgment. The Bible even says it "rages" against all wisdom. Rage is a strong word indicating force, violence, and even anger. It's aggressive, unrelenting, and destructive.

Why is sound judgment an area the enemy has targeted so acutely in our lives? Why is he so adamant and determined that we avoid it through the gambit of isolation? 2 Timothy 1:17 tells us that God has given us a sound mind. In legal terms, a sound mind means the ability to think, reason, and understand. The Greek definition of a sound mind (also called self-control in some translations) is "continuous reliance on the grace that God gives to individuals who trust Him implicitly.[13]"

Imagine being in a community where everyone is continually relying on the grace of God and trusting Him wholeheartedly, where He is our source of validation, trust, and self-worth. We would be able to

---

[13] B Gatley. (2020, June 27). A Sound Mind [Blog Post]. Retrieved from http:// www.briangatley.com/blog/06/a-sound-mind

communicate and interact with one another purely from a place of undefiled love. Love is the foundation of the two greatest commandments: to love God with all of our heart, soul, mind, and strength, and to love others as ourselves. My church's mission statement puts it simply--*love God, love people*. Sometimes we complicate the things God calls us to do. Even though it takes effort and intentionality, and may not always be easy, the two greatest commandments are not complex; they really are simple. We need to go back to the basics of what we are called to do--love God and love people.

God continually calls us to walk in love, and we learn what love looks like in 1 Corinthians 13, the "love chapter." One characteristic of love is selflessness. There is a quote that says, "Selflessness isn't thinking less of yourself; it's thinking of yourself less." Is our focus more on ourselves or on others and how we can love and serve them?

Realize that you not only need what others have to offer, but they need what you have as well. God created each of us with unique gifts, talents and abilities that can only be displayed best when we let Him use them for their intended purpose. Inquire of the Lord about what He has given you to build up others and be a blessing to those around you.

1 Corinthians talks about the body of Christ and how we are each a part of it, with our own specific functions and roles. We need to learn where we fit and what we are called to do, while also cutting the comparison and criticism we have towards other parts of the body. We have to be willing to work together in unity the way God designed us to.

No one can impact this world in the way that *you* can. Don't believe the lie that what you have to offer isn't special or needed, or that someone else can do it better. If everyone believed that what they possess isn't valuable, then no one would do anything. The world would be void of incredible inventions, melodious music, tasty treats, and brilliant books. Anything man-made that you enjoy can be traced back to someone's willingness to step out and use their God-given creativity to come up with it.

I always say that I am not artistic (trust me, I've unsuccessfully tried just about every craft project you can imagine), but I AM creative.

I write poetry, have comedic creativity, and am great at planning, vision casting, and executing ideas. We all are creative in our own, unique ways. I really believe it's impossible for anyone to not have some level of creativity within them; it just may be untapped or undiscovered. Creativity is a God-given attribute that we all possess, and even if we don't all function in the same ways or carry the same skillset, we all carry something valuable and important.

If you don't know what you carry that could possibly impact the world (whether that's the masses, your community, or a small group--the size doesn't matter), then ask the One who created you. James (New Testament book) tells us if we lack wisdom, to ask. It really is that simple and works in all areas of life where we seek wisdom. Grab a pen and paper and ask God to bring to mind what gifts, talents, and abilities He has given you and write them down.

I know God has given me a gift of humor. It's not something I have always embraced. I actually used to pray for God to take it away, which to most people probably sounds crazy! But now that I know it is a special gift, and that it benefits others when yielded correctly, I love it! Allowing God to mold my gift of humor is important. I am quick-witted, and most of the time my humor comes very off the cuff. It can easily be used (incorrectly) as a method to insult or injure others (and it has), but I want my gift to be used for good things. Besides, in everyday conversations, God has allowed me to use humor on social media through a comedy act I did with my sister for a while, as well as at a local theatre, a Christian country concert, and a women's conference. I want my humor to bless others and also help the underwear industry by making people pee their pants. Hey, maybe Hanes would even sponsor a comedy tour someday!

God has also given me a gift of communication. I love writing, and I love encouraging people. The gift of communication and encouragement has allowed me to easily develop good relationships with people and make others feel valuable and important--because they are! I really feel blessed to have some of the best friends and to be surrounded by people that have depth of character and deep passions in life. For me, building a relationship often starts with simply asking someone to go on a coffee date with me. That is honestly one of my favorite ways to get to know someone and have good, real conversation. I want relationships that exist outside of texting and occasional interactions.

Writing is a gift that God has used to serve others through my blog, social media platforms, poetry, and now this book. I can't remember a time in my life that I was not infatuated with writing. I still have diaries from elementary school. Although they're probably filled with unimportant information on my latest crush or friendship drama, I was compelled to write. Writing is a gift and passion God put inside me when He created me.

It's important for you to discover the gifts God created in you, because then you will realize more reasons why isolation is a trap. It will keep your gifts hidden, dormant, and isolated as well, never allowing others to experience the beautiful things that can only be shared by you.

Some gifts that God may have given you that you may not even realize are gifts:

Hospitality

Conversation

Servant-heart

Musical

Generosity

Artistic

Thoughtfulness

Cooking/Baking

Counseling

Administrative/Organizational

Reading

Writing

Mechanical

Outside of the Box Thinker

This list is a small fraction of God-given gifts that exist. It is inexhaustible in possibilities. An entire book could be created, and I'm sure has been, just about gifts. Romans 12:6-8 and 1 Corinthians 12:8-10 highlight spiritual gifts God gives, so take time to read those passages. I pray that even if my list above doesn't contain any of your gifts, that God reveals the ones He *has* given you, so that you can discover and use them for the good of others and for His glory. I also pray that you are filled with wisdom to use the gifts you have been given in the ways they were intended and created to be used.

I highly encourage you to read the book of Proverbs, even if you already have. There are thirty-one chapters, and a good practice is to read one each day that corresponds with the date (on the 1st, read Chapter one, 2nd, read Chapter two, and so on). Proverbs is the book of wisdom. The richness of God's wisdom is a deep, deep well, and He says it's for the righteous. So, absorb and receive all of the wisdom He has for you. As we receive and understand wisdom, it affects the way we see the world and interact with one another.

You will become like those you keep company with most. So naturally, I decided to join a Pilates class one time. And I do mean one time. I went and never returned. I thought it was a good idea, and never gave a thought to the potential difficulty of the class, until I was instructed to roll onto the exercise ball, and I immediately rolled right off the other side into an awkward ball of blubber on the ground. Being at the back of the class did not offer the ability to hide like I had hoped. My loud landing accompanied with a shriek and laughter left no possibility of hiding as the instructor left her spot at the front and came back to help me. I fumbled through the rest of the class, trying to avoid looking at my cringe worthy self in the surrounding mirrors. I continued going to the gym but skipped the Pilates class.

On a serious note, who we spend our time with really does matter, because they will either build us up or hold us back and sometimes even destroy us. I strongly encourage you to find a solid community that pushes and encourages you. Also, consider what you are contributing to your community. Is it edifying, encouraging, and life giving? If you don't have a life-giving community, pray for it.

Faithful are the wounds of a friend, but the kisses of an enemy are deceitful. — Proverbs 27:6

I want friends who love me enough to call me out and speak the truth even when it's not easy. I am thankful for the friends I have that do.

Stop thinking you have to have everything in common with someone in order to have a friendship with them. There is beauty in diversity. Some of my best friends are not my age, they're married or widowed, have kids, and are at a totally different place in life than I am. But those things don't matter because the foundation of our community is Christ. I love the gift of strong and diverse community.

What kind of community do I want most? A community where...

We cut the criticism and compliments are common.

Where lies are lost and truth is told.

Where we stop sabotaging one another and we boldly build each other up.

Where love is not limited or circumstantial or shallow.

Where the only words we speak to and about each other are life-giving words.

Where comparison and jealousy and gossip are eradicated.

Where we aren't afraid to be vulnerable and real and transparent.

Where we share our stories and see others set free and continue in that freedom.

Where we truly are the community God created us to be.

Chapter Ten

Free to Be Me

You are altogether beautiful, my darling; there is no flaw in you.
— Song of Solomon 4:7

Y ou are exactly who God created you to be. Your personality, the way you look, and even how you laugh are all ways you were wonderfully made. The single season is a perfect time to learn to love yourself and to truly fall in love with who God created you to be. Discovering who you are without the distraction of a relationship will actually make the future relationship God has for you even better. You are not replaceable, disposable, exchangeable, or forgettable. There only is, only ever has been, and only ever will be, one of you!

You were created and born to make an impact and difference in this world in a way that only you can. Your gifts, talents, and personality are as unique as your thumbprint, and they matter because you matter. There are so many deep truths about the beautiful person God created you to be, and my hope is that you become fully aware of and actually believe them.

This is something I am very confident and passionate about now, but I haven't always been. Growing up, three of the biggest insecurities (on my long list of many) were my weight, my teeth, and my hair. I have been overweight for the majority of my life. When my adult teeth came in, I looked like a half-bred human/shark. And puberty hit my body with a vengeance, turning my no-need-to-flat-iron, straight black hair into a frizzy ball of curls that looked like I had my finger permanently stuck in an electric socket. I would not have been surprised if my parents sat me down to tell me that I had been adopted from an alpaca farm--it was that bad! Middle school pictures are embarrassing reminders of the screaming flaws I allowed to label me as "not good enough."

The intense battle I faced when I looked in the mirror was dangerously destructive. My mind always tainted my reflection, slandering the girl I saw looking back at me. I was very skilled at slashing myself with a sharp verbal and mental sword of self-abuse. The way I thought and spoke about myself was very unhealthy and toxic. Those opinions were cruelly complemented by the voice of others. Their frequent negative words affirmed and intensified my own destructive beliefs about myself, making and keeping me feeling immensely insecure and shackled in my own skin. What a terrible feeling that so many of us struggle with!

One of my first childhood crushes reciprocated my short-lived feelings towards him with comments like "your fat" and other insolent weight-digging wisecracks. His comments weren't a solo act on the stage of my insecurity. In fact, they were more like one small part in a full orchestra, all perfectly playing the same tear-me-down tune. Other people I loved also spoke similar degrading words to and about my appearance. Unless you were completely blind, there was nothing I could do to hide the fact that I was the "fat" girl.

My mom would respond to my tear-filled heartache by telling me the age-old repetitive myth that I was just born with big bones. It didn't take me long to learn that having big bones wasn't reality, but I definitely commend her for trying to find a way to make me feel better about myself.

My adult teeth came in like an unshuffled, mismatched deck of cards. I had a giant gap between my front teeth. The teeth next to them were pushed really far back and my canines protruded. My entire mouth was an embarrassing wreck! And braces were too expensive for my single income family.

I remember wishing there was some sort of scholarship that I could apply for to get orthodontic work done. Without question, I knew I could prove that I was the world's worst-case scenario and definitely the most qualified for dental reconstruction. But no such scholarship existed to my knowledge, so I learned to master an excellent shut-mouth grin (at least for pictures).

When I became an adult, I finally had orthodontic work done. It is something for which I will forever be thankful. Proof of this is the fact that I still wear my retainer even after having my braces off for many years...who else can say that? It's difficult to even show a picture of myself with crooked teeth. And it isn't because I am embarrassed; it's because finding a picture of me smiling with my teeth showing is as impossible as fitting a shark for a bathing suit!

There is one very rare picture I do have from my sophomore or junior year in high school. American Idol did a tour with some of their top ten contestants from a previous season and made a stop near my hometown. I had watched that season faithfully, and my favorite contestant, George Huff, was part of the tour! I cancelled all of my plans, which included absolutely nothing, so that I could go with my dad and a group of friends.

I made a poster proclaiming my love and #1 fangirl status for George (you know, like you see on TV), and my friends made posters, too. It turned out no one besides us came with posters, but I didn't let that stop my excitement and enthusiasm. I proudly held up that poster throughout the concert, and we got invited backstage to meet George and the other contestants!

My picture with George is the cheesiest, most teeth-baring picture you will ever find of me.

Getting "before" pictures taken at the orthodontist was almost more painful than the weekly appointments to tighten my braces. I remember how incredibly awkward it felt posing with an open smile. Truthfully, I didn't even know HOW to smile with my teeth. If you check out my social media, you will discover that is no longer true. I never smile with my mouth closed anymore! Oh, what a world of difference it's made having my teeth shuffled to one row instead of two or three.

Then there's the hair. I learned to style my curly, alpaca like hair so that it wasn't an out of control mess on my noggin, but my insecurity was reawakened when an ex told me that he didn't like my hair curly and wished that I would flat iron it all of the time. Well, any curly haired girl who flat irons her hair knows that is not an easy or quick task. It's not only damaging to your hair, but it also makes your get-ready routine take way longer. So, a hair-tie became my best friend. I practically never wore my hair down and curly. If I didn't have time or just didn't want to flat iron my hair, it would get thrown into a sleek, old schoolmarm bun style.

As a teenager and young adult, wearing make-up was a chore that I saved for special occasions or periodic fun. It was never something I felt obligated to do. I've always had really nice skin and a pretty facial complexion, complete with perfectly rosy cheeks that were always mistaken for being painted with blush. I was truly always confident leaving my house without the need for pounds of makeup caked on my face, never even thinking twice about whether I should or shouldn't wear it. I was the girl who was "born with it" and didn't *need* the Maybelline. That sense of confidence was stripped away when (again) my ex let me know that he would prefer I not go out in public without makeup.

I could never understand why it always seemed like I was being defined solely by my appearance, because I had so many other amazing qualities! From a young age, I was smart and a quick learner, funny, and social, to name a few. It felt like any good qualities I had were buried and hidden under what "really" mattered (appearance), and that no one deemed my character qualities as worthy enough treasures to dig up. I quickly learned that a shallow world *can't* look deeper than the skin. My heart and my mind were marked at a very early age with the etching "not good enough." That beauty only meant appearance was a full-priced lie that I went bankrupt buying. I let the opinions of others, including the fear of their opinions, push me to wear unflattering, baggy clothes, change my hairstyle, force me to wear makeup, and hide my smile.

Of course, once the enemy has full reign on one territory of your life, he will go after anything else he can, too. Being confident in my appearance was a battle that I had no victory in, so the next place of target was my personality and other non-exterior qualities. I have always been a very quick-witted girl and funny without even trying. Sometimes *I* even laugh at the things that come out of my own mouth. I remember in second grade I would cry myself to sleep praying to God to *please* change my personality. I didn't like who I was and wanted to be like "the other girls." The enemy's MO never changes and comparison is a frequent trap he sets, especially for women. I struggled to love the extra extroverted funny girl God created me to be when He formed me in my mother's womb. (Psalm 139:13)

Some people are "extra." Well, I'm EXTRA extra, if you know what I mean (very outgoing, sometimes too loud, an extrovert with a capital

E). I have held back so much because I'm afraid if I show up as I really am, people won't like me, which is such a lie! I would rather be hated for who I am than loved for who I'm not.

The company I work for is a Japanese based manufacturing company. One day, our translator invited me to meet some Chinese members of one of our customers. I am unsure why she wanted me to meet them, because I have no direct dealings with our customers, and if my work was a totem pole, I'd be the portion of the wood below the ground. I am not in any sort of high-ranking position that would merit me meeting these individuals. Also, there was a huge language barrier because I speak zero Chinese and they spoke zero English.

I entered the meeting room like anyone would. Through the door. That's as far as I got on any level of normal. Beyond that, what happened was a perfect storm of uncontrollable and unbelievable events. I, for some reason, thought it was a good idea to display my kung-fu skills for the Chinese people. I thought "this is for sure a good way to communicate with them," while simultaneously thinking, "Why am I doing this?" and "I am pretty sure I am going to get fired for this." But their reaction surprised me, and also surprises everyone else when I share this story. They responded to my crazy kung-fu moves with their own native moves and taught me some new ones! They laughed and we shook hands. And even better, I didn't lose my job.

When we left the room, the translator exclaimed, "They loved you!" In that crazy, *I can't believe I just did that* moment, years of hating my goofy, silly, funny personality lost its power.

The last few years have really been an intentional journey to discover myself and be confident in who God created ME to be. Part of that has been learning to not be ashamed of my big, bold personality. Anyone with a big personality can probably relate to holding back at times or hesitating to be all that you are.

It is for freedom that Christ liberates us, and I believe that applies to every area of our lives: spiritually, emotionally, mentally, and physically. One of the ways I have found freedom in my life is to live fully into who He has created me to be.

I want to give you permission to be all that God created you to be!

Galatians 5:1 says that Christ set us free for our freedom, and that

84

includes all areas of our lives--our sin, insecurities, addictions, wrong thinking, and seeming shortcomings. There is nothing that Christ didn't and can't set us free from.

Freedom is "the power or right to act, speak, or think as one wants without hindrance or restraint." The second part of this verse in Galatians tells us to "not be burdened again by a yoke of slavery." The bondage of always conforming to the expectations of others, seeing myself through muddy glasses, and believing less about myself than what God thinks and says, is a place I no longer live in.

The day my curls found freedom is a day that marked my life. After I became single and my confidence started to be restored and rise, I made a bold and gutsy decision. I resolved to wear my hair down and curly--in public. Walking into work, my mind screamed at me as I put one foot in front of the other, thinking of nothing else but the way my hair looked. I expected someone to criticize or say something sarcastic about my curls, because that's what I was used to hearing. I had believed the lie that they weren't pretty enough, so I didn't think anyone else would think otherwise either. And I thought that if I at least expected the chiding, when it came it wouldn't hurt so much. Then the first fated comment came. "Janice, I LOVE your hair!"

Instead of the expected ridicule and mockery, I was met with a sincere compliment. The insecurity of my curly hair that was weighing me down broke off me in an instant. I didn't need multiple people to validate this with their statements. I just needed that one person to see me the way God created me, a girl with bouncy locks, and to love myself for it. Since that brave day, I have continued to wear my curly hair unashamedly. And the compliments haven't stopped either.

More recently, there was a day that my curly hair was a total tangled and tameless mess. I am pretty sure when I used hairspray that morning that I somehow missed my head completely. My boss told me that my hair was 'kinda all over' on my head. I chuckled and the words did not upset or bother me one bit! Then I went to the bathroom. As I washed my hands, I looked in the mirror and gasped. She wasn't kidding. My hair was absolutely wild on my head! I laughed and said out loud, "Wow, I look like the bride of Frankenstein!"

Despite my outrageously wild tresses, I did not put my hair up (although the thought crossed my mind). I chose to wear it down as a statement that it doesn't matter what my hair looks like. What does matter? How I feel inside.

***

That I laugh uncontrollably more often than I ever have in my entire life.

That my laugh is so loud and obnoxious, but I have decided not to hold it back anymore.

The way that I treat people, and how they feel when they are around me.

Dancing and singing with joy in my heart, without caring who sees or hears me.

Letting others know that they are valid, they matter, and that they are beautiful.

I don't remember ever hearing someone tell me that I am beautiful until I was around eighteen. I'm not saying that no one ever thought it, I just don't recall hearing it. My friend and Mary Kay director broke the eighteen-year record and told me I was beautiful. I didn't even know how to respond to her. I thought it was an absolutely ridiculous thing to say. So, I laughed and said something like "yea right." It took me a while, and hearing it many times, to become the girl who now tells other people that *they* are beautiful. Because it's true. We are all fearfully and wonderfully made, fashioned together perfectly by the Creator of the universe.

Insecurities make us feel ashamed. One definition of ashamed is being embarrassed because of one's characteristics. A characteristic is "a feature or quality belonging to a person and serving to identify it." Too often, we allow what others say about our characteristics to define how we, too, feel about them, even when their opinions have no foundation of truth whatsoever.

One of my favorite books is "Unashamed" by Christine Caine. This book helped me journey through so much deep healing and to experience lasting freedom. I love that Christine uses her story coupled with the truth of God's Word to help readers find and continue walking in the freedom Christ paid for with the ultimate sacrifice. The tagline for the book is "Drop the baggage. Pick up your freedom. Fulfill your destiny." We all have a calling in our lives, but the things we carry can weigh us down and hold us back. Jesus came to set us free in all areas of our life, including how we feel, and what we believe about ourselves from the inside out. The description on the back of the book says, "This book will help you learn, or relearn, how to define yourself by God's truth, and your life will begin to take shape as it was designed to be." I share this with you because it did exactly that for my life. I repeatedly endorse this book and buy it for my friends, because it helped me learn to love who I am.

And it's about time we all begin to love who we are. Who we truly are. I shared this analogy with my middle school youth kids.

Suppose you have worked really hard on a hobby you love and are deeply passionate about such as art. You have created wonderful masterpieces of all kinds: paintings, murals, drawings, sculptures, photography, and more. Too many to mention in even one sitting. You decide to open a museum to display all of your art because you have so many incredible pieces that you are proud of and want to share with the world. You know and understand the value of what is on display and see no reason to keep the good works to yourself. The work is tedious, time consuming, and not easy, but you know it's worth every ounce of effort.

The long-awaited day finally arrives for you to open the museum to the public. To your shock and dismay, the people you've welcomed into your space begin destroying your artwork. They rip paintings off the wall, smash the sculptures, and demolish artifacts one after another. They see no value in any of the work you created and, not only do they verbally share their dislike, they seek to ruin every piece of art in the place.

Imagine how you would feel--sad, frustrated, even angry. I believe this is a glimpse of how God feels when He sees us destroying His masterpieces--His people. The Bible says we are God's handiwork, (Ephesians 2:10) but how often do we really see ourselves or others as such? My heartfelt prayer is that we actually realize the way our words and actions impact each other. And that we not only realize the power of our words and actions, but that we also choose to use them intentionally to speak life and truth as we allow God to open our eyes to the value of His beautiful creations.

Our intrinsic value is worth far more than rubies. God places the price tag on us and only He can write on that tag and declare our worth accurately. He is your Maker and He determines your value, and that worth is much higher than any human-determined value could ever merit.

Stop letting other people put their faulty appraisals on you. Resolve (decide firmly) to allow God to change how you view yourself and others. Ask God to show you how He sees you through His Word and His voice in prayer. Refuse to speak or let the negativity you hear settle in your heart. Stop being afraid of living your life loud and loving who you are. It doesn't matter if you are a size zero or a size one hundred, how many chins you have, or if your waistline has surpassed the muffin-top status and is more like a busted can of biscuits. It doesn't matter if you have one, two, or five rows of teeth, or no teeth at all. It doesn't matter if your hair is long and straight, short and curly, or if you choose to wear it in a mohawk. You can be an introvert, extrovert, or a somewhere in the middle ambivert. You can be so funny you make yourself pee from laughing or have a sense of humor drier than the Sahara Desert. You can be academically astute or more skilled in street smarts and common sense, or a little of both. You can have the best corporate position or work for minimum wage. Your appearance, personality, social, and economic status are small fractions of who you are. What does matter is that *you* matter, and with certainty I can tell you that you truly are altogether beautiful.

Chapter Eleven

Pledge to Purity

Create in me a clean (pure) heart, O God. — Psalm 51:10a

Get lost in your purpose and chase purity. —Michael Todd

Purity is a battle we must persistently engage in. God has given us the exact weapons we need to win the war through the power of the Holy Spirit and His Word. The fight for purity feels like a lone feud at times, but there are many who have pledged to make purity a priority in their lives. Even though it's often counter-cultural and unpopular, we must tenaciously pursue purity in all realms of our lives.

What is purity? The definition of purity is "freedom from adulteration or contamination." Sin contaminates us, but Jesus' sacrifice of His own life cleanses the stains of sin and gives us the victory over and freedom from it. There is no sin too dirty for Jesus to clean. 1 Corinthians 15:57 says, "But thanks be to God, who gives us the victory through our Lord Jesus Christ." 1 John 1:9 is a promise I am forever thankful for: "If we confess our sins, He is faithful and just to forgive us our sins and to cleanse us from all unrighteousness." The Gospel really is good news, and we have to be careful to not overcomplicate it.

It may seem like a taboo topic, or even like an old-fashioned thing to talk about, something that is no longer relevant in today's world, but we need to courageously have more conversations about purity. Even though it's where our minds tend to hesitate automatically when the topic of purity is brought up, it is a much bigger discussion than just sexual, although that is definitely a part of the conversation.

Whether we have given it little thought, or already asked God to help us in this area, we have to know that the Bible has a lot to say about purity, and the Word of God will always be relevant in the life of a believer. Adhering to the scriptures is much more than a form of obligatory behavior modification to appease a higher power. It's about desiring to live in a way that honors God, knowing that any instruction He gives us is always with our best interest in mind.

We, as humans, are composed of three parts: body, spirit, and soul. Our body is our physical makeup. Our spirit is our eternal being--the part of us that will live on forever. The soul is made up of our mind, will, and emotions. The heart is described as the seat of our soul, and the two terms are often used interchangeably. So, when we talk about purity of heart or soul, we are talking about the area of our mind, will, and emotions. Jesus taught that sin almost always starts in our minds, which then results in our outward actions. He likens lust to adultery in our hearts and equates hatred to murder. To attack purity, we have to begin with waging war in, what Joyce Meyer calls, the battlefield of our mind.

God never calls us to do anything that is out of the realm of possibility. Purity is possible. Psalm 119:9 tells us that we can stay on a path of purity by living according to the Word of God. Colossians 3:5 instructs us to put impurity to death. Matthew 5:8 says the pure in heart are blessed. His believed and applied Word purifies our hearts and minds and results in blessing. I pray this chapter serves as a funeral to impurity in your life as you are charged to live according to the Word.

I once heard someone say, "purity is inward out, not outward in." What he meant is that purity is a work of the Holy Spirit that happens inside of us first and then shows outwardly in the way we behave and act. Our own "good" actions and behavior don't have the ability to clean us inside, rather they should be an outward expression and evidence of an internal work that has already been done.

One of the very best ways to pursue purity, and something I have done in my own life, is to acquire an accountability partner. This has to be someone you can trust and are willing to be vulnerable with; someone who will pray with and for you and hold you accountable to live by the standards of God's Word. They will encourage you and correct you in love when needed. You will also do all of these things for them. Pray about finding this type of accountability partner. If and when God brings someone to mind, boldly reach out and talk to them about it. This may look like checking in once a week, meeting up monthly, or emailing every other day. There is no set way it has to be done, just do what works for the both of you.

Purity is important when it comes to any relationship you decide to pursue beyond friendship. Take this time to set a godly standard and expectation, and don't compromise it. The value of your life is not contingent upon your relationship status and being single is not the end of the world, even if it feels that way sometimes. Being in the wrong relationship is a much worse scenario (trust me), so please don't rush into a relationship flippantly. This is a great topic to discuss with a trusted mentor, or your accountability partner. I recently sat down with one of my best friends and talked to her about what it is that I desire in a future spouse, and I know that she will pray for me and hold me accountable to not settling.

Have people in your life that you trust to "screen" any potential person of interest who comes along your path. They will be able to see without the rose-colored glasses that sometimes limit your own sight. That doesn't mean we are trying to find the "perfect" person, because such a person doesn't exist, but we have to be willing to hear outside voices when it comes to one of the biggest decisions of our lives. With prayer and wisdom, they can help make sure the person is right for you with more of an objective eye and that they are truly God's best. I strongly urge you to not enter a serious relationship with anyone without hearing what trusted outside voices have to say and weigh in on the pairing. Also, continue the dialogue with outsiders as the relationship progresses.

We live in a culture of tactless Tinder-like hook-ups, consisting of self-seeking, ignorant, and emotional decision making based on whatever feels good in the moment. We engage in fleshly momentary match-making with precarious regard to purity. We dangle the idea of serious commitment on a string, likening the idea of locking it in with someone permanently to being in a prison. The product of these kinds of asinine actions is heartbreak, confusion, and unhealthy soul ties.

Even Christian culture errs on the side of compromise way too often. We settle for sex outside of marriage, or at the very least push the envelope to see how far we can go without going "all the way." Too often we tread the line to see how close we can get before it's considered "sin" instead of seeing how far away from the line we can get and stay. I don't say these things with a condescending tone. I say them with complete understanding because I have fallen into these traps myself, and so have many people that I know and love. Compromise is like mislabeled poison disguised in a bottle of your favorite drink. It may taste good at first, but the inevitable results are anything but good.

1 Thessalonians tells us that part of God's will for us is to abstain from fornication. Fornication is any kind of sexual activity outside of marriage. The word fornication comes from the same root words as "furnace, oven, to burn." The fire of sexual desire is a natural part of the way we are wired as humans, but to fornicate is to mishandle that fire. It's a perversion of the appropriate place for the heat, which is within a marriage covenant.

The problem happens when that fire within us isn't correctly contained. Think of marriage as a fire pit or fireplace. Those are safe places for a fire to kindle and burn the way it was intended to. Outside of marriage, it's like lighting a match and flippantly throwing it on the ground. The uncontained fire has the ability to damage anything within its ruthless path of destruction. When sex is unbridled outside of marriage, damage happens.

For too long, the enemy has tried to taint and destroy the beauty of sex through the wiles of perversion. God created sex, and it has its perfect place within the context of a marriage relationship. It was God's great idea and mandate to mankind from the beginning of creation. I mean, think about it. It was the first thing He told Adam and Eve to do after creating them. It was His idea, His design, and His desire for covenant couples to enjoy a satisfying sexual relationship with one another.

Repeatedly in the Song of Solomon, the writer, King Solomon, charges readers to not arouse or awaken love prematurely. It should be noted that King Solomon is considered the wisest man in history, so we would be wise to incline our ears to his teachings.

One of my best friends wrote a beautiful song based on these verses in the Bible and sang it on her wedding day. The lyrics say, "Awaken my love, for the time has come." She knew and understood the value of saving herself for her wedding day and not allowing desire to awaken prior to the day she made that commitment to her now husband.

Purity may seem like a dated word, but it's not. As our world grows increasingly crude, purity is progressively demeaned and defended less. It goes completely against the grain of society and what we are taught in the majority of our homes, classrooms, and on mainstream media. Our sexual cravings are labeled as a healthy way to relieve stress or something to enjoy recreationally, and who we fulfill the need with doesn't matter as long as the need is being met. We are told to practice safe sex to avoid STDs and unplanned pregnancy, but the voices that warn of the emotional and spiritual repercussions of flippant sexual activity are usually stifled or silenced altogether.

There are plenty of reasons to justify compromising our sexual purity. We may feel like we truly love a person and intend to spend the rest of our lives with them anyway, so why does it matter? We may have already given our virginity away, so waiting seems pointless now. Or maybe we just enjoy the recreation of sex and feel that as long as no one knows, we use protection, and we don't get pregnant in the process, then we are safe.

If you have treated sex flippantly, I challenge you to begin guarding your heart and fighting for purity. Your body and emotions are worth protecting. Even if you plan to spend the rest of your life with someone, until you say, "I do," you are not in a covenant with them yet. God's mercy can cover any areas of past compromises, so if you have already been sexually active, you can start again with a fresh slate.

As a young teen, I remember playing spin-the-bottle many times. To my own embarrassment, the worst experience of that nerve-racking juvenile game involved me spinning the bottle and having it land on my biggest crush. My excitement ended when I aggressively pulled him in for a smooch, completely missed his lips, and planted a big kiss on his nose. No do-over, just an awkward exchange of looks and him exclaiming "you kissed my nose!" ended that round, and made my cheeks turn redder than a bowl of my favorite tomato soup. A close second to that horrific story involved the time I kissed a boy and actually *did* land my lips in the right place. The satisfaction of my bullseye lip-landing accuracy was squashed when he told me I kissed like a woodpecker.

A game that seems like innocent middle school fun opened the door for me to begin devaluing even the cost of a precious kiss. I allowed someone to pay the cheap price of a bottle-neck landing in my direction in exchange for a kiss that I can never get back. Some might argue that it's "only a kiss," but when did we start throwing our kisses on a clearance rack, it's like they are worth nothing.

As a single woman, I am very careful and cognizant of the music I listen to. Desires that cannot be met during this season of my life have to be carefully guarded and kept dormant. The last thing I should do is spend my time listening to sappy, sensual love songs. Compromise begins in the mind and causes impurity without even carrying out the actual act, as I mentioned earlier. God is pretty straightforward in Scripture about the seriousness of our thought life. If we find that something, such as the movies we watch or music we listen to, causes us to stumble, then the solution is simple--avoid it.

After going through a divorce, it was very easy for me to fall into the trap and believe the lie that I cannot be pure again. I want to encourage you that, if you have had sex, whether within the context of a previous marriage or outside of covenant, God is a God of redemption and restoration. He can take away the pain of old memories and bad decisions. Through Him, all things can be made new, and you can be pure sexually. You are the bride of Christ, and His bride is without spot or wrinkle.

Undamaged

Unadulterated

Uncontaminated

Pure and holy

I know many people who compromised their sexual purity in the past but then chose to abstain from sexual activity outside of marriage and pursue purity. God honored that commitment by giving them a sense of newness, like the compromise had never even happened. God wants to restore you and allow you to see yourself the way He does-- clean.

Lyrics from one of my favorite Natalie Grant songs called "Clean[14]" helped me heal so much during the aftermath of my divorce:

I see shattered, You see whole,

---

[14] Grant, Natalie. "Clean." *Be One*, Curb Records, Inc., 2015. MP3.

I see broken, You see beautiful,

and You're helping me to believe,

that You're restoring me piece by piece

There's nothing too dirty,

that You can't make worthy,

You wash me in mercy,

I am clean

These beautiful words magnified the love of God and His ability and willingness to make me whole again in every way. The anointed lyrics destroyed yokes of bondage that were holding me captive in my heart and mind. God's goodness sought after me, a very broken and hurting young woman. He was completely unafraid to deal with the damage that had been done in my life. God is not intimidated by heartbreak, destruction, and impurity.

Jesus reached out often and touched those who society discarded and labeled as impure. No one had a condition He was unwilling to come close to. He opened blind eyes, cleansed lepers, and healed the lame. He didn't always wait for them to come to Him, He frequently sought them out. He modeled perfectly what it means to love people. God never sees us as disposable.

Another song that has really ministered to me and helped me heal is "Beloved" by Jordan Feliz[15]: "Forget the lies you heard, rise above the hurt, and listen to these words, You are beloved." Music has a magnificent way of ministering to our hearts. Anointed with the truth of God's Word and saturated with His love, it has the ability to break through devastation and destruction and combat even the most deeply rooted lies. Strongholds crumble when confronted with truth.

I encourage you as you pledge yourself to purity and fight the good fight of faith for it, to also pray for those around you, both married and single. We inevitably see the demolition caused by infidelity, adultery, and fornication as it wreaks havoc in the lives of those around us. The strongest and most upstanding people have fallen. It's heartbreaking,

---

[15] Feliz, Jordan. "Beloved." *Beloved.* Centricity Music, 2015. MP3.

and it's worth investing our prayers in.

I also urge singles to pray for the purity of their future spouse. Pray against any strongholds of a sexual nature, as well as healing and restoration from any past situations. Pray that your future spouse desires purity and commits to abstaining from sex until your wedding day.

Take time, whether you're married or not, to construct boundaries that will enable you to "avoid the appearance of evil," (1 Thessalonians 5:22) as well as avoid possible traps. One example of a boundary I have established in my life is that I do not allow an unrelated man to be in my home when I am alone. This determined boundary has been set before I enter a relationship and will help me avoid temptation down the road when I do have a boyfriend/fiancé. I know married men who will not allow themselves to be alone in the company of a woman. Some call it extreme, I call it wisdom. As a woman, I admire men who possess those kinds of standards.

I encourage everyone to check out Havilah Cunnington's ministry called "Moral Revolution" (www.moralrevolution.com as well as social media platforms[16]). This ministry is equipping our generation with teachings, videos, and more on relevant and sometimes hard to talk about topics. Havilah is a trusted teacher of the Word, and I gladly endorse her ministry as a godly resource to others.

Pornography is an epidemic that is infiltrating our culture. It's luring promises of satisfaction and enjoyment are actualized with addiction, abuse, and unrealistic expectations. The difficult pill to swallow is the fact that many in the church have been entangled in the trap of pornography, including ministry leaders and even children. One great resource for anyone looking for accountability in this area is an app called "Covenant Eyes." It monitors your internet activity with the help of someone you trust. This requires vulnerability but winning the battle of purity is worth being real with someone about your struggle.

There is a scene in the movie "Fireproof" where the lead character battles a pornography addiction. Finally, he gets serious enough about gaining freedom from it that he takes his computer outside and clobbers it to smithereens with a baseball bat. This may seem extreme, but how serious are we willing to be when it comes to purity and being

---

[16] Moral Revolution. www.moralrevolution.com. www.facebook.com/ moralrevolution

faithful to honor each other and God?

James 1:27 says that part of having a pure and faultless religion is to keep us from being polluted by the world. *We stay pure by remaining unpolluted.* Does the way we talk and act mimic Christ, or look more like the world? How do our ambitions and motives look--pure or polluted? I want to love God so much that I am willing to take a stand, even if it means I am standing alone. I want my speech to be full of grace, seasoned with salt, full of words that edify, encourage, and benefit those who hear them. I want to speak and act in line with the truth and not let the enemy have a hold on any area of my thought life, my speech, or my actions. To do this, I must be serious about guarding my heart.

One of the greatest gifts I will be able to give my future husband is all of me. Not a hurting, destroyed, fragmented version of myself, but a healthy, whole, and healed me. The version of me that God created. As I end this chapter, I dedicate it to the man that I will someday marry. Babe, I am committing myself to pursuing God in all areas of my life while I wait for you, and I am pledging myself to purity.

Chapter Twelve

A Cause for Celebration

Whoever trusts in the Lord, happy is he. — Proverbs 16:20b

You will show me the path of life; in Your presence is fullness of joy; at Your right hand are pleasures forevermore. — Psalm 16:11

God's plans for us are good. The Bible says we cannot even fathom the things He has prepared for us. (1 Corinthians 2:9) I believe that includes both during this momentary life, and also what awaits us beyond it into the rest of eternity. As a child of God, I want all that He has for me. I don't want to forfeit any of the good things that are mine simply because I belong to Him. His goodness, grace, and mercy are not things we have to strive or work for, they are simply received.

That's a hard concept to understand in a world where nothing is free and most things have strings attached. We give to get. There is always an exchange of something in order to receive anything in return. Most religions are works-based, making followers strive and work towards achieving anything from their god. Christianity defies that method. Ephesians 2:8 tells us that the salvation God gives us has nothing to do with us (our works, efforts, good deeds) and everything to do with the price Jesus paid. It's a gift of grace that we receive by faith alone.

Jesus gave all He had, His very life, so that we could receive all He has for us--eternal life, blessings, and restored relationship with God that had been broken as a result of sin. He paid the wages of sin (death) that we could not afford, so that we could freely receive eternal life. (Romans 6:23) "Blessed be the God and Father of our Lord Jesus Christ, who has blessed us with every spiritual blessing in the heavenly places in Christ." (Ephesians 1:3) Every promise and blessing is for every believer. That makes me want to throw a party and celebrate!

Life doesn't always give us a burning desire to celebrate, though.

98

Even when it sometimes seems like the easier or only option is sitting and sulking, it's a waste of the precious gift of life God has given us. We were not created to live defeated, pessimistic, and down-trodden. Feel free to eat the most delicious confetti cake with the thickest frosting and globs of colorful sprinkles, and bring me a piece of it, but don't throw yourself a constant pity party parade. God can restore and redeem every short stick, bad hand, and unfair situation that has beset you. Your life can have a fresh start, regardless of anything that happened in your past.

In the Gospel book of Luke, we read about the Parable of the Prodigal Son. He asked for and received his inheritance early and chose to sinfully squander all that he was given. After he had nothing left to live on, he bravely chose to return home with the expectation of losing his status as a son and becoming a hired hand. His father met him while he was still a bit far off, covered him with his own robe, put a signet ring on his finger, and threw a party--quite the opposite response of what he had anticipated. The father showed him what true love looks like. It is unwavering, unfaltering, and unchanging. Bad behavior and stupid choices didn't stop the father's love. The only way the son missed out on all that the father had for him was when he chose to forfeit it; all he had to do was return home to receive the good things the father had for him all along.

This is a parable that grips my heart as I realize it displays the immense love of our Heavenly Father. I am also obliged to point out the response of the prodigal son's brother. He was upset and angry that he had never left home but had never been thrown a party and shown love the way his irresponsible and foolish brother had. The father reminded him that he had access to all of those good things the entire time; he just hadn't realized it. The Bible says that Heaven throws a party when someone repents and turns to God. (Luke 15:7) So, whether we are a child who has run off like the prodigal son or has "forgotten" what is rightfully ours like his brother, I pray that we return and stay home and fully experience all that our Father God has for us.

Sometimes we focus so much on the big blessings in life that we lose sight of the smaller ones, which are just as significant. When I was a teenager, I went to a Kelly Clarkson concert with some of my friends. Schick was sponsoring the tour and, at the exit doors of the venue, they had giant boxes of free razors. These were like luxury razors to the girl (me) who always bought the cheap disposable ones. The worker handing them out told us that we could take as many as we wanted. Since I thought they might scold me if I hauled out the entire box, and I didn't have any sort of bag, I loaded my arms up with as many as I could hold. I didn't care how stupid I looked, because the value of what I was taking home was higher than my concerns about my appearance.

The treasures that God has for us should mean more than anything else, too. And just like the Schick razors, God always has something much better to offer than the cheap, disposable things we often settle for. Yet a lot of times we allow the fear of man and the need to guard our reputation to hold us back. We are afraid to ask someone to pray for them because they may reject us. We resist lifting our hands during worship because we fear what an onlooker may think of us. We don't speak up when we should because we are concerned about what others may think if we do. We carry gifts and talents that lay dormant within us because we are so afraid of rejection, disapproval, and opinions of other people. My prayer is that you stop letting what other people think hold you back and that the fear of man be broken in every area of your life.

We have to stop constantly focusing on "what's next" because, when we do, we are missing out on what God is doing "right now." Psalm 68:19 says, "Blessed be the Lord, who daily loads us with benefits, the God of our salvation!" Psalm 23:6 says, "Surely goodness and mercy shall follow me all the days of my life." Every morning that we are granted to open our eyes, His mercies are new. Every single day, He doesn't just give us some good things, He LOADS us with benefits. He withholds no good thing from us. There are countless good things He has for His children, and I pray that we realize and appreciate every single one of them.

Sometimes as a single person with no potential prospects, the last thing you feel like doing is celebrating. What is there to celebrate? Another Valentine's Day #solo? Another Christmas with no one to stand under the mistletoe with? A really great milestone or life event and no one to share it with?

I totally understand the pangs of loneliness and wearying feelings of being left out that sometimes come with being single. Our eyes can

100

choose to only focus on the fact that we are surrounded by people that have everything we are (often impatiently) waiting for--a spouse, children, a home to share with someone we love, family vacations, and memories of our own to behold. Our mind can ruminate on all that we wish we had and don't.

Or we can choose to celebrate!

What does it mean to celebrate? Good ol' Webster defines the word celebrate as "acknowledge (a significant or happy day or event) with a social gathering or enjoyable activity."

Throwing a bash for your single season is unheard of and kind of absurd. Who does that? It's just not normal. Sure, let's have a party for singleness. I'll be the first in line to smash the colorful piñata with a broomstick, especially if there are tootsie rolls inside! And if tacos are on the menu, I'm for sure there! But wait, what exactly am I celebrating? The list of what is worth celebrating is wildly endless. What in your life, right now, exactly where you are, can you celebrate? Seriously, stop and think about it. Name three things about your life that have absolutely no bearing on a relationship status that you can praise God for!

I don't believe in giving a challenge I am not willing to take on myself. So here are my three (it's hard to narrow them down!):

I am celebrating the opportunity to speak at my first conference next month.

I am celebrating the journey of getting healthy in all areas of my life.

I am celebrating friendships that inspire and challenge me.

Life does not begin and end with a relationship. One of the biggest challenges that I have willingly faced happened a few years back when I entered a weight-loss competition. I had joined a women's only fitness center with my sister and had started making the gym a more frequent scene. When they announced the weight loss competition, I had no interest in joining. My sister, also known as my personal cheerleader, offered to pay my entry cost, so I signed up reluctantly. For several weeks, I tracked every calorie and made eating healthy and exercising a top priority. Each week's weigh-in was a celebration of the hard work I was putting in as the pounds kept coming off. By the end, I had little competition as many of the contestants quit or lost their drive and commitment to the process. I won the competition and was awarded bragging rights and a cash prize, but more than that I was given better health and every girl's dream--the need to shop for new clothes. My focus, determination, and drive pushed me to finish the contest and take first place.

Our focus, determination, and drive-in life has to mean more than momentary accolades and achievements, though. For singles, the constant focus of a seemingly never changing relationship status has to shift. Drudging in our flighty feelings can drum up insecurity, jealousy, sadness, and depression. The fear of always being single drives us to desperation. A lot of times we end up on a dead-end road that only leads to bad decisions and settling. We have to stop seeing singlehood as a prison sentence and start loving all of the good things that it brings. We have to look for and find purpose in the single season.

I love this quote by Lysa Terkerust[17] and I tell it to myself often:

You steer where you stare.

So, what is it you are staring at and fixing your attention on? In Philippians 4:8, the apostle Paul gives us a list of things to think about. This list is applicable whether you are single, dating, or married; it's for all of us. I encourage you to train your mind to think about these things, just like the scripture encourages.

Whatever is....

True

Noble

Right

Pure

Lovely

Admirable

---

[17] TerKeurst, L. (2018, December 11). We Steer Where We Stare. Retrieved from http://lifewayvoices.com/culture.../we-steer-where-we-stare/

Excellent

Praiseworthy

We have a choice where we park our attention. We can choose to wallow in what we want and don't have, or we can be thankful and praise God for what we do have. Reminding ourselves of His promises and His character helps settle our hearts and reminds us that He is trustworthy. He instructs us to have anxiety for nothing, so we have to be sure we guard ourselves against it because it's less than God's best. We were not created to carry the weight of the world, even our own little world. So, choose today to let go of the burden of the "when, how, and what-if" questions and rest in Jesus as He carries the load for you.

Ultimately, this life really is so short, and I don't want to spend my days wasting away on the sidelines and feeling like I am only "in the game" when I have someone by my side. I am not benched, and neither are you my friend!

So, shift your focus to what really matters in life. See the sunrise and celebrate the sunset. Learn to laugh and dare to dance. While you have breath in your lungs, breathe in deeply and don't take one moment of this precious, beautiful life for granted.

The struggle with maintaining a mind frame of peace is nothing new. Look back to the Old Testament prophet Isaiah who wrote simple, but not always easy to follow, instructions for us to keep in perfect peace. (Isaiah 26:3) How do we do it? The answer is by keeping our minds "stayed" on God. To stay means to remain in the same place. Don't let situations or circumstances, or even what is happening in the world around you, move your mind off God. When you do, you will lose that place of perfect peace. Jesus is the Prince of Peace, and there is no source outside of Him that can produce authentic, lasting peace.

We can always back the unknown variables of our future with God's promises that will never change. Read the promises in Scripture such as, "He is able to do exceedingly, abundantly above all that we ask, think or imagine," (Ephesians 3:20) and "No eye has seen, no ear has heard, nor has it entered into the heart of man what God has prepared for those who love Him." (1 Corinthians 2:9) The best part? God wants you to hold Him to His word. He wants you to actually believe what He says!

I have told Him many times, "God, You do realize that I have a very creative mind. I can imagine some pretty incredible things for my life. So, if You are going to do bigger and better than that, I am going to dream even greater." I am sure He just smiles and thinks, "Oh girl, you truly have no idea what I am going to do in and through your life."

We have to intentionally fix our focus on the season we are in now and not allow ourselves to get so caught up in what may or may not lie on the road ahead. We must allow God to order our steps and let ourselves experience the places our feet are landing right here and right now. Choose to celebrate the current season and find the beautiful blessings this season holds, because when we look for those blessings, we absolutely will find them.

We don't have to know every little detail of our future. Fear of the unknown, fear of disappointment, and the unnecessary need for control pushes us to press for more information, leaving us frustrated when we are left with little or no specifics. Most times, I do wish I knew more about what lies ahead on my life's journey, but where is the element of surprise in that? Faith is the substance of things hoped for, and the evidence of things unseen. (Hebrews 11:1) The opposite of faith isn't fear, it's sight. We don't need faith for anything we can see. I want to walk by faith, hoping and believing for things that seem too lofty, unrealistic, and impossible.

I have always loved birthdays, especially my own. I have passed the point of celebrating for one day and have taken it to the extreme by making it a month-long celebration. I am not sure what I love most about birthdays--the attention, the gifts, the reminder that God has given me life--probably a combination of all of it and then some.

I remember many details of my past birthdays throughout the years and what made them unique and special. When I turned ten, I raised my hand during class at the exact time I was born to let everyone know it was officially my birthday. For my fourteenth birthday, my grandma made banana flavored pancakes for breakfast and took me roller-skating. On my sixteenth birthday, I skipped school with my best friend and my mom took us out to eat at a buffet for lunch. I ate so much that I made myself sick. I got as far as the bathroom door and puked all over the floor. That was embarrassing. As a single, I have had friends throw me parties, and a few years ago I threw my own birthday party. Yes, you read that right. I decided to decorate my house, have a taco bar (my favorite), and invite my best friends over to celebrate. I think celebrating ourselves is fun and important, even if it's unusual.

Throughout the years, I have had many parties, countless cards, piñatas, dinners, outings, and songs sung to celebrate the day God chose to give me life. We can have the same joy that birthdays somehow seem to bring any day of the year.

One prayer that I pray often is "thank you God that You rejoice over me with singing and that Your banner over me is love." I think too many times we view God as this distant deity that sits behind a big podium with a giant gavel constantly ready to slam it down with every wrong move we make. But Scripture says He rejoices over us with singing. (Zephaniah 3:17) Singing indicates joy. In His presence is fullness of joy, (Psalm 16:11) and joy is a fruit of the Holy Spirit. (Galatians 5:22) Joy is an expression of God's character. I believe God actually smiles. That is an image not everyone has of Him because religion has incorrectly painted Him to be mean, critical, stern, and unloving. I encourage you to read the Word and ask God to reveal who He truly is to you, and not just believe He is how others have portrayed Him to be.

When I was a kid, I loved going to the Dollar Tree, and my favorite thing to buy was always the surprise bags. They were simple brown paper bags filled with items that I'm sure they were unable to sell otherwise--junk that no one wanted. I stood in the aisle and felt the bags, usually with no good or accurate guesses as to what was inside. After finally selecting and paying for my surprise bag, I would euphorically rip it open, never expecting anything great inside, but almost always enjoying a good laugh by the random revealed contents.

The idea and fun of getting a surprise surpassed the near certainty of getting something I didn't even want (which happened almost every time). I was willing to gamble my dollar, not even because I would want or benefit from what was inside the bag. I just loved the thrill of the unknown, the celebration of the surprise! I want to be more excited for the life God has for me now and in the future than I was about all of my dollar store surprise bags combined. I know that what He has in store for me now and on the road ahead is not useless, random, or meaningless. His plans for me are good, and His plans for you are good, and that is worth celebrating.

Chapter Thirteen

Coruscate the Crown

An excellent wife is the crown of her husband. — Proverbs 12:4a

Who can find a virtuous wife? For her worth is far above rubies.
—Proverbs 31:10

Weddings are a time of celebration and unity that has crossed traditional and cultural borders throughout the entirety of human history. The uniqueness and beauty of a holy union is a gift straight from the heart of God. Marriage is sacred, and the purposes within a holy covenant are endlessly deep and vast. A time of two separate paths of life colliding together to form one united pathway; two individuals officially becoming one in every aspect--physically and spiritually. The motive for matrimony is both outward and upward, painting an earthly picture of the heavenly covenant between Christ and His church, affectionately called the Bride of Christ.

The Bible tells us that Jesus will one day return for His bride, the church. This is what we call the "second coming." The parable of the ten virgins told by Jesus in Matthew 25 is a message for the church to be ready for Him when He comes back. I encourage you to read it and soak in the truths found in the message. Ask God to show you how to be like the wise virgins portrayed in the parable, and avoid the mistakes made by the foolish ones. Even though we don't know the day or the hour Jesus will come back, we can prepare and keep oil in our lamps by making our relationship with Him a priority. Intimacy and first love passion is a must in the life of a believer. I don't want to be found foolish, squandering my time and attention on things that don't really matter. I want to be ready when He comes back.

There are also wise and foolish ways to prepare for an earthly marriage. It's imperative that we prepare for the marriage more than the wedding day. So much time, effort, and money go into making the most of a one-day celebration, often at the expense of not even enjoying the day ourselves. Women can unintentionally turn into notorious "bridezillas," forfeiting feelings of joy and elation for stress, impatience, and frustration. We spend a fortune and exhaust ourselves in order to impress others for a day that is not even about them, yet often fail to prepare for what actually matters, the marriage itself.

I am not saying we should negate planning and preparing for our special day. Have a blast sending out invitations, picking out your colors, and hiring a DJ to dance the night away. I am certain my wedding day will be full of fun, love, laughter, and tears, but I am committing now to make my wedding day first and foremost a celebration of the pledge I am making before God and others to my significant other.

I want to spend more time, effort, and energy investing in the long term, the time beyond my wedding day. The joy of my wedding day is something I want to always be able to look back at with fondness and delight, but I don't want my marriage to start and end on my wedding day. I want to build upon the vows exchanged, and always look for ways to grow through love and serving. I desire a marriage built on a firm foundation that is unshakeable, unwavering, and stable in every way.

Preparing for the marriage is something that can, and should, start within singlehood. Know your worth and stop giving discounts to others. Don't cheapen who you are. Don't remove your expensive price tag and throw yourself on a clearance rack. Don't let anyone else put you on a clearance rack either.

You are excellent. That sounds like a pretty high, even unattainable, standard. But don't skip this chapter, because it's not!

What does it even mean to be an "excellent" wife, and how do you become or find one? Some of my favorite synonyms for excellent are *exceptional, outstanding, awesome, mind-blowing, fantastic, admirable, and matchless.* Read those words again.

If you're a woman, know with confidence and certainty that you can attain these attributes. If you're a man, these are characteristic traits to desire and look for in a woman. If you are taken and not even "on the market," you can still strive for excellence in your own life and encourage a high standard in the lives of those around you. No matter what relationship status you find yourself in now or in the future, allow God to develop your character and exchange worldly traits for

Godly, Kingdom-like ones.

As believers, God calls us to carry and bear His light in this world. I believe that is one of the best ways to be excellent--to exemplify Jesus in our daily lives. After all, the Bible says that we are to be like Him and to conform to the pattern of His image (check out 1 John 4:17 & 2 Corinthians 3:18). Don't hide the beautiful light you carry. Boldly display your light to bring Him glory and to show hope to a lost and broken world.

You are the light of the world. A city that is set on a hill cannot be hidden. Nor do they light a lamp and put it under a basket, but on a lamp stand, and it gives light to all who are in the house. Let your light so shine before men, that they may see your good works and glorify your Father in heaven. —Matthew 5:14-16

I refuse to believe that God made us to be mediocre. Consider the process of creation and the fact that God literally created everything by simply speaking. Psalm 33:6 says, "By the word of the Lord the heavens were made, and all the host of them by the breath of His mouth." The universe and each individual star were formed by the simple, but mighty breath of God! God said, "Let there be light," and there was light. (Genesis 1:3) He breathed His breath into the dust and created man. (Genesis 2:7) Think about the countless animals and plants that exist because He chose to create them. John 1:3 says, "All things were made through Him, and without Him nothing was made that was made." Nothing about the creation process is lame or mediocre, so I adamantly refuse to settle for ordinary or be less than He created me to be.

So how do we 'coruscate the crown,' and what does that word even mean? Coruscate means (of light) flash or sparkle; to shoot forth bursts of light. Some other fun related words are shimmer, glow, shine, dazzle, and radiate. To coruscate is to shine, so let's let our crowns shine brightly!

Who God created you to be is an absolute blessing to the world, and also for the person He purposes you to be with. Take time to seek God and ask Him to reveal all of the beautiful purpose-filled attributes He created you with--your gifts, talents, abilities, personality, and more. Knowing fully who you are and walking confidently in your God-given identity will make your "crown" shine brighter. A crown is a symbol of royalty. There is humility and honor that come with the status of royalty. Jesus, our Savior, is the King of kings, the ultimate representation of such.

The Bible calls us righteous, which means we are in right standing with God. It's not a result of anything we can do to earn it; it's the beautiful finished work of the cross that makes righteousness possible. **Know who you are in Christ, because if you don't, I guarantee you will live less than you were created for.**

Here are some truths for you to settle in your heart sweet reader:

You are chosen.

You are loved.

You are valuable.

You matter.

Your story matters.

Your life matters.

You matter.

Sometimes we have a hard time seeing past who we have been, and the mistakes we have made in life, to truly believe that we could be a valuable adornment to anyone, let alone to God. Proverbs tells us that "he who finds a wife finds a good thing." (Proverbs 18:22) It's a mistake to think that verse applies to everyone else *but* us. The Bible in its entirety is written for every believer, so if you have a hard time believing you could be (or find) a "good thing," ask God to stir and increase faith inside of you.

The Word of God is not a buffet; we can't pick and choose which parts of the scriptures we want and don't want. He is an all or nothing kind of God. His entire Word is true, so if He calls us chosen and loved, we are chosen and loved. What we believe about ourselves matters, so choose to begin (and continue) believing the truth of what God says about you.

Past pain can tarnish the way we see ourselves. We have to heal from anything in our past that hinders us from seeing the true, intrinsic value of who God created us to be--fearfully and wonderfully made.

We have to be intentional to replace any lies that have taken root in our hearts, even unintentionally, with the truth of who we *actually* are in Christ.

One of my favorite lady preachers, Real Talk Kim, has a quote that I love[18]:

> *Heal so we can stop accidentally hurting people we want to love because we are projecting our own wounds on them.*

Real Talk Kim was instrumental in my life and journey through healing post-divorce. A friend sent me a clip of her doing a live video from her car. Little did I know this beautiful sister from Georgia would impact me so deeply. I began to watch all of her videos, listen to her sermons, and read her first book. She was so encouraging and listening to her breathed life back into me. I had the honor of meeting her in person at a women's event a few years ago, and I was able to tell her the impact she had on my life. I think it's special to let someone know when they have ministered to you or affected your life in positive ways. As someone who is now on the other side of healing and using my own story to minister, it's encouraging to know when my story helps others.

Jeremiah 17:14 is a verse that I believe with my entire being: "Heal me, O LORD, and I will be healed."

After my divorce, I wanted nothing more than to heal and be whole again. I knew before I ever entered another romantic relationship, I had the responsibility of letting God deal with the damage that came with being so broken. And trust me, I had a lot to let Him deal with. There were times I didn't even feel like I owned a crown at all, much less a tainted one. Spiritually speaking, I saw myself with rags on, matted hair, and mascara-stained cheeks from the countless tears I cried. Even in such despair, I knew God would exchange my heaps of ashes for beauty. Praise God that He is so loving, patient, and faithful, able and willing to heal us, and make us completely new and whole. We never journey alone, because He never leaves or forsakes us. Even in our times of most devastating brokenness when we feel completely abandoned, He is with us.

---

[18] www.minerals.net

There were several ways I journeyed through healing and learning to step more fully into who God created me to be. Some of this may be similar to what was shared in the "Heal the Hurt" chapter, but I believe some things are worth repeating. The first and most important thing I did was make Bible reading a priority in my life. The Word of God has the power to transform and change us in unfathomable ways. I also became intentional about spending time with God. I love turning on worship music and lying on my living room floor praying. Prayer consists of pouring my heart out to Him and also allowing Him to speak to me. Sometimes no words are exchanged, just the beautiful birthright as a believer of being in His presence.

I also have been very purposeful in surrounding myself with people who build me up, speak and live truth, and invigorate my life. I put a note card on my fridge (it's still there today) that simply says "Jehovah Rapha," which means "the Lord who heals." It is my continual reminder that I serve a God who heals, and I had faith from the beginning that He would heal me. Counseling is a great way to find healing, and even a great way to navigate through life in general. I had an amazing counselor, Janelle, who became a very good friend through grieving the loss of my marriage. There are some incredible counselors out there, and don't be ashamed to schedule an appointment to meet with one.

The journey of healing is an excursion for some and a voyage for others; it doesn't look the same for everyone. Allow God to map out your journey and don't get caught up comparing your route to anyone else's. The process of "shining the crown" looks different for all of us, but the beauty of becoming brighter is an objective we can all fight for.

When people give advice, chew the hay and spit out the sticks. Ask God to give you discernment regarding things spoken to you--what is true and needs to be applied; what is not true and needs to be discarded. Don't feel obligated to believe everything you hear and be okay with setting up healthy boundaries to guard your heart. There are seasons of life where certain people are just not good for you to be around. That sounds harsh, but it's true. I want you to "prosper and be in good health, just as your soul prospers." (3 John 1:2) To prosper is to thrive, flourish, and bloom. Way more than I do, God desires that for you.

The word "excellent" used to describe a wife in Proverbs indicates an immeasurable core value. It's not a merit based on what we *do*, it's based on who we *are*. I want to be a woman of high value, and I pray other women reading this have that same desire. I also pray for men to rise up and be someone who has a high standard of excellence and desires a woman with the same. The value placed on a monarchy's royal crown is of such high value that it actually is deemed invaluable. There is no price tag high enough to adequately monetize the value of a royal crown. That is the same for you. You are so valuable and worth so much that no price tag could display a number high enough to accurately read your worth. One version of Proverbs 31 says that the worth of a noble woman is far more than rubies. Rubies are known for their high value and equally as high for their rarity. Let's choose to be known for the same.

The pursuit of believers should be a continual process of holiness (in the language of "Christianese" this is called sanctification). The more we read and apply the Word of God and surrender our lives to Him, the rarer we, as a "crown," become. Allowing Him to be Lord over every area of our lives means that we give Him access to everything and nothing is off limits. We transform from the pattern of the world into the image of Christ as we renew our minds. (Romans 12:2) He is the only one who can bring deep and lasting change within us.

I love the saying that "God loves us where we are, but He loves us too much to leave us that way." Isaiah 61:3 says He will give us beautiful exchanges--a crown of beauty for ashes, oil of joy for mourning, and a garment of praise for the spirit of heaviness. Our ashes are our mistakes, our regrets, the shame and pain of the past, and anything else that has, or ever will, hurt us. This is the God who willingly exchanges our ugly messes for better things. Oh, how I love Him!

What do you want to be able to say you accomplished while single to prepare yourself for marriage and make your crown shine brighter? I want to reiterate that my journey belongs to me, and yours won't be identical to mine or anyone else's. However, we can certainly learn from each other and incorporate things that work for us. This is just a warning filled with love to not get caught up in comparisons. It's ugly and accomplishes nothing of eternal value.

One way that I have already shared, but want to share again, that we can be intentional to coruscate our crown is by guarding our heart. The Bible says that above all else, more than anything, to guard our heart. It's that important. It's that valuable. It matters that much.

Three gateways to the heart are our eyes, our ears, and our thoughts. I don't promote perfectionism, but I do advocate for holiness. I hate legalism (doing things out of stringent obligation), but I do love honoring and pleasing God. I guard my eyes by being mindful of what I put in front of them. I don't watch shows that dishonor Him or are below the standard of life He calls me to live. I guard my ears in a similar way. I am cautious of the music I listen to, the voices I allow to speak into my life, and my own voice. Why would we want to indulge in things that promote a lower standard purely for entertainment's sake?

The last gateway is one we don't always take into consideration. What is your own voice saying? Are you speaking truth or coming into agreement with your adversary? I strive to guard my thoughts like 2 Corinthians 10:5 tells us to, which is to "take every thought captive unto the obedience of Christ." The way you live your life is a direct result of your thought life. Proverbs 23:7 reminds us that "As a man thinks, so is he." You really are the sum of your thought life, so take time to evaluate it. I used to believe a lot of lies about myself, and I had some friends bold enough to challenge me to repent from coming into agreement with those lies, and to speak the truth of what God says in place of them. I challenge you to do the same thing.

During the past few years of my single journey, I have aspired to live with Godly intention regarding dating. I refuse to mindlessly date. The market of men that capture my interest is extremely miniscule; but even the few that do meet my standards must be filtered through prayer. If God tells me "no" when I pray about someone, which has happened, then it's settled. I'm pretty black and white when it comes to relationships. I don't have time to waste on purposeless relationships, and I only want to give my heart to the one God has for me.

I want my future husband to know that even now while I am still single and have yet to begin a relationship with him, I value and honor him. That I allowed God to do a work within me to become the wife he deserves. That my affections and attention are reserved fully for him. My heart's desire is to walk down the aisle on my wedding day and present my husband with a beautiful, brilliant, pure, and radiant crown; a crown that he will be proud to wear because it coruscates so brightly.

114

Chapter Fourteen

Attention Undivided

The unmarried woman cares about the things of the Lord, that she may be holy both in body and in spirit. — 1 Corinthians 7:34 (partial)

The place God calls you to is the place where your deep gladness and the world's deep hunger meet. — Frederick Buechner

Momentous growth happens in the areas we give the most attention. Our mind is like a train, and it will progress on whatever track we let it get on. We must evaluate the destination our thought life is taking us to and derail from any tracks that compromise truth. We have the ability to let ourselves off the train at any point by building stopping stations in our mind; points where we refuse to go any further on the tracks and choose to get on another train and go a different direction.

When our mind wanders in worry, we can stop the train and redirect it to the faithfulness of God's promises and provisions. When we are steering in fear, we can reroute to a track of power, love, and sound mind. When our thoughts are consumed with complaining, frustration, and annoyance, we can shift to thoughts of thankfulness and ruminate in gratefulness instead.

We have a choice where we allow our attention to park. While single, we can focus on all that we want and don't have, or we can ask God for a fresh perspective on all of the blessings the single season holds and celebrate them. Let's face it, relationships take time and effort. Having a season of being single affords us the ability to have laser beam focus on our relationship with God and the ability to grow in knowledge of the Word without distraction. It is also an ample opportunity to grow in any areas we are passionate about.

I want my single season to be consumed with knowing Him and making Him known. To chase after things that matter to me. To make and crush personal goals. To run my race well and live a life that magnifies the Kingdom of God.

Don't wait until you change your relationship status before you choose to really live. What can you do with the time you have right now when a relationship does not need any of your attention? I want to be clear that I don't make having a relationship sound like a prison sentence, because I believe God has so many beautiful purposes within a marriage. I do, however, want to empower you to live a life of fullness whether you're in a relationship or not.

One of my biggest passions in life has always been talking. Women reading this are most likely muttering "relatable," while men are thinking "of course, you're a woman." I do find it interesting that women speak an estimated four times more words per day than men. Most women just have an innate desire and need to verbalize everything, but I know there are men that do, too. My dad breaks the mold of men as being someone who talks virtually nonstop. While many women push their husbands to talk more, my mom begs my dad to stop.

With the passion and gift to speak, probably inherited from my dad, God has given me the ability and opportunity to host my own podcast show "Just Janice," which has been a fun adventure. My podcasting journey started with the inspiration of Jamie Lyn Wallnau's podcast called "Set Apart." The purpose of Jamie's show is for listeners "to be uncompromisingly set apart with God in every sphere of influence and experience an abundant life He designed for each of us.[19]" Jamie's show is so anointed and inspiring; I encourage everyone to listen to it. Her desire to live and inspire others to be holy and set apart unto the Lord is also my desire and the heartbeat of this book.

Finding an outlet for our passions is something we should be prayerful about, and that can look different for each of us. I don't believe God gave any of us gifts that are meant to lie dormant and never be used. It's unsettling to think about the number of incredible gifts God has given His people that are never realized or that remain uncultivated because of fear or failure to find an appropriate way to use them. The chance to discover and cultivate the gifts within us in an

---

[19] Wallnau, J. L. "Set Apart with Jamie Lyn Wallnau." Anchor. MP3.

unhindered way is a gift during a season of attention undivided.

Have you ever been on a phone call and realized that you have completely zoned out from the conversation, and you are nearly clueless as to what the person on the other end of the line is talking about? I have done this more than I care to admit. My feeble attempts to chime in with an appropriate response is usually successful, but there have been times I have said something that was totally irrelevant and made no sense whatsoever. This has happened to me because my attention was averted from the words that were being spoken by the other person. I was not hearing and comprehending what was being communicated because I let my mind wander from the conversation and my focus was fixed elsewhere.

When the role is reversed and I am the one speaking words that fall on deaf ears, it can be very frustrating and upsetting. I have been in conversations where I have realized that, while I may have a face looking at me while I'm talking, I do not have their full, undivided attention. I can see in their eyes that their mind is a million miles from the mutterings of my mouth. It makes me feel like what I am sharing isn't worthwhile or meaningful, even if it is.

I was challenged a few years ago to learn to really listen when someone is talking to me. Part of the challenge was to learn to listen in order to *hear* what is being said versus listening to *respond*. I thought listening was one of my better skill sets, until I actually paid attention to the way that I listen. I realized that I was often not truly hearing what was being communicated. I wasn't paying attention fully to the words spoken, let alone body language, which is also a very important form of communication.

In an effort to empathize, I often reverted conversations back to myself and took the focus off the other person. I realized that while I wanted to have meaningful dialogue with others, I unintentionally made most conversations about myself. Learning to keep the focus on the person in front of me, while offering personal insight as needed and not as a primary response, is a form of wisdom I want to walk in continually. Also, it's important to not jump ahead in my mind to what I'll say next or to be thinking about how I should respond. Sometimes wisdom is even saying "I don't have a response, but I hear your heart." Not forcing conversations, and letting them flow naturally, contributes to effective communication.

I desire to have meaningful conversations, and I have learned to truly listen to what is being communicated by constantly maneuvering my mind and making it stay focused on what is in front of me--the person who is sharing their heart and the words that are proceeding from their mouth.

I want to have this same undivided attention with the Lord. I want to hear what is on His heart and what He has to say without always trying to steer the conversation in the direction I think it should go. I want to let myself park in His presence and just listen with my mouth shut. I want to say things like "tell me more," as I navigate the privilege of getting to know the heart of my Creator. He has so much to say, but how often do we actually listen to Him?

In any season of life, we have the amazing privilege of offering God our undivided attention. In 1 Corinthians 7:35, the apostle Paul tells us that he doesn't talk about remaining unmarried in order to put a leash on us. He isn't trying to hold the unmarried person back at all. The latter part of the verse says that without a relationship, we are able to "serve the Lord without distraction." Relationships take work--there is no question about it! While single, we should relish in taking full advantage of the privilege of serving the Lord without the distraction of a relationship.

Marriage is not forbidden or condemned at all in Scripture. In fact, there are many passages in the Bible about the beauty of marriage. I am not implying that we should forget our desires to be in a relationship and neither does Paul. I do, however, want to give a charge to take advantage of the time you have during a season of singleness to focus solely on the most important relationship of your life--your relationship with God.

It goes without saying that attention is divided when we are in relationship with someone. It should be. Our partner deserves our attention, time, and loyalty. God desires for us to have deep, meaningful relationships with other people and to flourish in the relationships He blesses us with. But don't rush into a relationship with someone as an attempt to abandon feelings of loneliness. I want you to know that you can live a very full life during your single season, and the ability to enjoy a fruitful life has nothing to do with your relationship status. I can say that confidently, because I have been single for over four years now and have experienced a very full and fruitful season of life.

Attention undivided can look a myriad of different ways because the path God has laid out for each of our lives is as unique as our individual fingerprints. Learn what it means for you to be holy in body and spirit as you care for the things of the Lord.

One of my most favorite lady preachers, Susanne Cox, shared about her season of being single at a conference I attended while I was still married. It amazes me that her teaching was brought back to my remembrance so many years later and ministers to me now during my season of singleness. I remember her sharing about how she scheduled dates nights with Jesus. While her friends were getting together and socializing, she uncompromisingly resolved to spend her Friday nights getting to know the Lover of her soul.

I am a very busy person and I like to keep my calendar filled with coffee dates with friends, traveling, having people over (hello hospitality, I love you!), and ministry opportunities. It didn't take me long to realize that, while my plans may be fun and fruitful, I cannot fill my calendar at the expense of intimate time with God. I remembered Susanne's story, and early on in my single season I began to carve out evenings where I refused to put anything else on my calendar. I quickly realized how many things were vying for my attention when I had to start saying "no."

I heard a quote one time that said, "If the enemy can't stop you, he will try to push and hurry you." That is so true in my life. I enjoy fast-paced living. I thrive on setting goals and meeting deadlines. I am an excellent multi-tasker. The enemy is hard pressed to get me to sit down or shut up, so instead his method to destroy me (see John 10:10) is to push me to move faster than I should, get me to take on more than God has intended for me, and to get in a cycle of hurry where I am so busy that I don't get the intimate time with God that I desperately need and He so very much deserves.

One of the many beautiful things about having a season of attention undivided is the fact that I can create my schedule without having to take someone else into consideration. I want God's full wisdom to know when to adamantly say "yes" and when to respectfully say "no." It's still something I am learning, but for now I can plan my life with only One person to take into consideration. I know that this lesson in time management will ultimately be a blessing when I do mesh my life, and calendar, with the man God has for me.

And those nights where I don't plan anything with or for other people, but only with and for God, have become precious to me. Last summer I found that one of my favorite things to do is sit on the hill behind my church while reading my Bible and writing in my journal. I love that the plans I can make with Him do not always have to look the same or ever become monotonous. I don't serve a boring God, so getting to spend time with Him shouldn't be boring either.

Another thing that I have learned to love during this time is writing scriptures. I love writing, and I value knowing the Word of God. One of the best and easiest ways for me to learn and memorize the scriptures is to write them out. My good friend, Jessica, got me a Write the Word journal for my birthday last year. Each page has a Scripture reference. I start by looking up the passages, reading them (usually out loud), then writing them out on the page. I'll reread the passages then journal my takeaways and what God is showing me in the text. His Word really is alive and active, and it can have such a vital role in our lives, if we allow it.

Other times, I will just open my Bible and write out verses in one of my many other journals. I also love sending people happy mail and writing them a portion of Scripture in a card or sending texts to my friends with Scripture. Encouraging others, especially with the Word, is such an honor. I encourage you to do that for someone today!

For a few years, I was able to focus my attention and time on middle school students on a weekly basis. Teaching students the value of God's Word, what it means, and how to implement it into their everyday lives was a blast. Ministry is done by married couples every day, and done well, but the ability to lead a ministry as a single woman will forever be one of my favorite accomplishments during my single season.

The Bible calls all believers "ministers of reconciliation." (2 Corinthians 5:18) While you may not be called to lead a ministry in the same ways I or others have, you *are* called to the ministry in some form or fashion. Your ministry may not be a group of middle school kiddos every week (many of you say hallelujah to that!), but it could look like the gal who sits next to you at work, the young man taking your caramel frappe and large fries order at McDonald's, or the elderly person greeting you at Wal-Mart. Pray for God to help you to be a minister in the world wherever He has placed you.

Don't be so distracted by the busyness of life that you miss the opportunities He puts right in front of you. I don't like praying for God to give us opportunities to minister, because I believe any time you have a person in your pathway, you have an opportunity. I believe a better prayer is for God to open our eyes to the opportunities we often overlook, and for an extra dose of boldness and courage to accomplish the things that are on His heart for us to do.

A season of attention undivided is a gift. I pray that you open it and explore its contents fully. Ask God to show you all that He has for you during this season. Learn to hear His voice clearer than you ever have. One of my favorite verses that I remind myself of often is John 10:27. It's Jesus telling us that His sheep hear His voice. In times when others doubt if God still speaks to His people, or even when I question if I am hearing from Him, I remember this verse and the fact that God cannot lie. If He said it, it's a truth check I can take to the bank and not worry about it being returned due to insufficient funds. He has more than enough in His proverbial account to back every promise He issues.

The best way for me to know that I am hearing Him is to not neglect my time in the Bible. I am a firm believer that the Bible is just as relevant today as it was when it was written. Sadly, this belief isn't a very popular one, as many have dubbed it irrelevant, outdated, and unneeded for our world today. If you have not made Bible reading a priority, or even given it a thought, I lovingly challenge you to take time to read through the book of John in the New Testament. It's a great place to start, and it's all about the life of Jesus Christ. I know many people who have learned to love God in new and deeper ways after reading this beautiful book. I know it's changed my life!

The more we get in the Word of God, the more we learn the character and heart of God, which consequently leads to a deeper love and intimacy with Him. Then, when we believe God is speaking to us, we can test that voice by a few things: does it line up with the Word of God, and does it line up with the character and heart of God? God will never contradict His written Word, so we must base what we hear against it. Then it's simple. If what we hear goes against Scripture, we know it's not God speaking, so we reject it. If Scripture supports what we hear, we receive it and respond accordingly.

Another way to dig deeper in relationship with God and learn His voice better is to spend time in prayer. I love playing worship music while I pray. There are times where I pour out my praises to Him and pray for a myriad of things on my heart and mind, but it's just as crucial that I zip my lips and allow Him to speak to me as well. He is the lover of my soul, and I desire to hear what He has to say.

For me, I know when God is speaking because I hear what I would describe as a really loud thought. Some people hear God audibly or in other ways. How we hear God isn't that important; what matters is that we are hearing from Him and that we recognize when He is speaking. The ways God communicates are endless. Sometimes He speaks a loving word of correction, sometimes it's a word of encouragement, sometimes it's direction regarding something we are called to do or say. He is a good Father, and He has things to say to His children, so let's open our spiritual ears to hear Him speak.

Recently, I was spending some time praying throughout my house and declaring that my home is a place that I want His presence to feel welcome and to dwell. I asked God to show me if there is anything in my home that isn't pleasing to Him. He brought to my mind a specific DVD that I had, and I knew it meant that it contained compromising content. I found it and took it out to my trash receptacle.

Another time during prayer, God put on my heart to send a letter every day for thirty days to one of my friends and encourage them with a note and Scripture. "Yes Lord," was not my immediate response at all, because I thought it would be awkward, and I wasn't sure what my friend would think (hello, Proverbs 29:25 in action). A few weeks went by and my attempt to ignore what God was asking me to do failed. I finally chose to be obedient and follow through with what God put on my heart, and for thirty days I wrote encouraging words and scriptures and mailed them to my friend.

I am not going to say being obedient is always easy, because it's not. It requires something of us--a willingness to lay down our pride, time, resources, and convenience. The Scripture says that He delights in our obedience, and that it is better than any sacrifice. More than anything I have or do during my life time; I want to please and honor Him with my obedience. I want to be a girl who says "Yes, Lord" without hesitation. I want Him to continually show me ways that I can be more set apart, as well as ways I can be a blessing to other people.

Being single is the perfect time to allow God to shape and mold you and make you more like Him. The Bible says that we are continually being conformed into the image of God. (2 Corinthians 3:18) Sanctification is a beautiful exchange of becoming less like the world and more like our Creator; the way we were always intended to be. God created mankind in His image (checkout the account of creation in Genesis). After the fall of mankind, we became tainted by the sin that entered the world. That was all reversed by Jesus (also known as the second Adam), and now there is a way for our image to be restored through acceptance of Jesus Christ as Lord and Savior and having a relationship with Him.

John 17:17 is a very special prayer because it is one that Jesus prayed to the Father for us as believers. It makes my heart burst with excitement and thankfulness that Jesus prayed for me before I was even alive on this earth. Read the whole seventeenth chapter in John, and you can hear what else He prayed for us--for YOU! Verse 17 says, "Sanctify them by Your truth. Your word is truth." Sanctification, becoming more like Him, will take place for the rest of our lives, and I encourage you to allow God to begin that work in you now.

If you've already ventured out and started the journey of being sanctified and set apart, I encourage you to keep going and don't stop letting Him work in your life. If you've lived a lot of your life without letting God fully in, know that it's never too late to start the process. God will always meet us exactly where we are at, whether that's in a church building, our kitchen, a work cubicle, or at a local bar. Nothing and nowhere is off limits to the God who passionately pursues His people. He is always ready and willing to start and continue a life-changing relationship with us.

God always has us on His heart and mind. Psalm 139:17-18 reveals that God's thoughts toward us outnumber the grains of sand. I can't imagine trying to count the number of grains in just a simple handful of sand, let alone every grain that exists on the face of the earth. It's literally impossible. God's thoughts towards us are innumerable; too many to count. Jeremiah 29:11 gives us a glimpse of those many thoughts and reveals that they are peaceful and full of hope. Our finite minds cannot grasp the immensity and depth of His lavish love, and even though I can't fully comprehend it, I want it and I receive it every single day.

Learning to walk in newness with God is a gift He gives us and something we can grow in daily. Ephesians 4 and 5 are great chapters to read about what newness of life looks like. Scripture can act as a mirror if we let it. When we read it, we should examine ourselves against what it says. It's never to condemn us, but rather to correct us and shape our lives in the best ways possible. James 1:22 says to not just listen to the word but to actually do what it says. Let's always encourage one another to get into the Word and apply it to our lives. Let's spur one another on towards love and good works. (Hebrews 10:24) Let's choose to live set apart unto the Lord in every way, especially while our attention is undivided.

Chapter Fifteen

First Love Passion

Pursue love. —1 Corinthians 14:1

Nevertheless, I have this against you, that you have left your first love. —Revelations 2:4

There is something so special about the feelings of newness that accompany the start of a relationship. The object of our affection consumes our time, occupies our mind and captivates our attention. We willingly and gladly invest ourselves in the relationship, because it means so much to us. Our heart is wrapped up in the other person's well-being as we find our own enhanced by their very presence in our life. They say falling in love is easy but staying in love takes work.

Newness is something we never want to lose. We purchase sprays to keep the colors vibrant on our clothing, schedule Botox injections to keep our faces looking young, and we trade in our perfectly running vehicles for the newest models. As a culture, we are obsessed with the latest and greatest of everything. We need new and are always looking for ways to pursue it.

My heart is to leave a legacy that points to the love of God that consumed my life here on this earth. I think about the countless people in Scripture and throughout history who forsook everything to follow Jesus: the twelve disciples, the ones that journeyed with Him from city to city, the women that supported His ministry from their own resources, and even my pastor who abandoned his own plans of a career in sports medicine to go to Bible college and enter the ministry.

I love **Steffany** Gretzinger's song called "No One Ever Cared for Me Like Jesus." The lyrics portray the desire of my heart and all that I want to be known as for loving Jesus.

If my heart could tell a story

If my life would sing a song

If I have a testimony

If I have anything at all

No one ever cared for me like Jesus

His faithful hand has held me all this way

And when I'm old and grey

And all my days are numbered on the earth

Let it be known in You alone

My joy was found[20]

In a world where everything around us seems to compete for our time, attention and affections, maintaining a first love passion for God can be challenging. One prayer I have had during my time of being single, and even more so recently, has been for God to stir in me a first love passion and desire for Him again. I never want my love for Him to grow cold and complacent or fall from the position of first priority.

I remember when I first fell in love with God. I was seventeen and attending a small youth group in my hometown. This was the same small town I attended from preschool all the way through high school graduation. I had a childhood full of vacation Bible school, released time Bible class, and Sunday school memories, which all served as fuel for the desire to know Him more.

I finally gave my heart completely to God after a Wednesday night youth group service. I don't remember anything specific about the service itself, but I do remember my surrender to Jesus as Lord in my car afterwards. I cried as I realized I wanted more than casual and infrequent encounters with the God of all things. The incredible, personal love of God and the realization I had of my complete need for Him in my life impacted me deeply and changed me forever. I made a decision to not just know *about* God but to actually know Him.

---

[20] Gretzinger, Steffany. "No One Ever Cared for Me Like Jesus." *Forever Amen.* Provident Label Group, 2020. MP3.

As I grew in my faith and understanding of Him through sitting under sound teachings and reading my Bible, I wanted others to know about the radical love of God that had put a permanent mark on me and was gradually changing me into the person I was always meant to be. My pastor always challenged us to share the Gospel and find ways to evangelize, and I fully accepted the challenge. I shared about Him with anyone who would listen--my family, friends, classmates, coworkers, and even complete strangers. I would go out looking for people that I could speak with about God. My love for Him was so immense, and it motivated me to do things that only love could compel me to do.

Ruth is one of my favorite people in scripture. If coffee dates are a thing in Heaven, I want one with her. She was a woman whose story is told in just four short chapters in the Old Testament. Her life was marked by a bold decision to leave her familiar homeland and relocate to a new place with her mother-in-law Naomi. She chose to abandon the gods of her homeland and serve the One true God. Ruth was not a woman who lived in idleness, and her resolve to move resulted in her being in the direct lineage of Christ. Her decision is such a strong example of surrender to God's plan, and the beauty that comes when we relent our own will to His. Love compelled Ruth to leave the only land she ever knew and embark boldly into the unknown future God had for her.

One of my biggest fears in life has always been heights. Acrophobia has had a grip on me for as long as I can remember. My grandma has told me more than once about one of my kindergarten field trips that she helped chaperone. Apparently, there was an escalator we all had to take at the museum we were visiting, and I was so scared that someone had to carry me on it. I have no recollection of this happening but, based on other past experiences involving heights, I have never even questioned the validity of the story.

In 2007, I had the opportunity to join several youth groups, along with my own, on an AIM (Ambassadors in Mission) mission trip to the Dominican Republic. We were invited to help missionaries, Matt and Carrie Love, for several days doing service projects and outreaches in very poverty-stricken communities. My eagerness to walk through every door God opened for me superseded my extreme fear of flying, and I decided to raise the funds to go.

The night before our departure from the Detroit airport, I barely slept. The sounds of airplanes taking off and landing all night long was unsettling. My stomach was in tight knots and my mind screamed every possible (illogical) reason I should not get on that airplane and just go home. I was still pretty young in my Christian walk and hadn't learned yet the power of taking my thoughts captive and speaking words of faith.

Even though my mind raced like a Sunday morning Nascar tournament, I was determined to not let fear stop me, and I got on the airplane with a feeling of dread. My apprehension literally skyrocketed and, as we took off, the unfamiliarity of flying, coupled with my unfounded fear, gripped me tightly. The crippling anxiety that came over me felt completely out of my control. I shook nervously and began to (quietly) cry. Once I realized the plane was staying in the air and was not going to suddenly drop out of the sky as I had imagined, I was able to relax and actually even enjoy the flight.

Why would I do something that completely scared me senseless? The best answer I have to that question is an echo of 2 Corinthians 5:14: the love of Christ compelled me. Since I gave my life to God, I have done things I never thought I would do, and He has taken me to places I never thought I would go. The love of God motivated me to travel almost two thousand miles to tell people in poverty-stricken villages that there is a God who loves and wants a relationship with them. It has also driven me to share His love in my own community and any place He has put me since that first life-changing love encounter.

Love will do that. It compels us to do things we may have deemed impossible at one time, or at the very least thought to be extremely unlikely. It compels us to speak up and take a stand for what's right. It compels us to silence ourselves to forms of hurtful speech (gossip, slander, negativity), because we know and understand the power of our words and would never want to damage someone with them. It compels us to action when the result is worth the pursuit and worth fighting for. 1 Corinthians 13:8 speaks the truth that "love never fails."

Definitions of the word fail include:

1. *Be unsuccessful in achieving one's goals.*

2. *Neglect to do something.*

3. *Break down; cease to work well.*

Because love never fails, we can confidently know it does the opposite of anything linked to failure. Love *is* successful in achieving one's goals. Love does *not* neglect to do something; it tends to and maintains care for the object of its affection, refuses complacency, and spurns sitting still when action is necessary. Love does *not* break down or cease to work well; it is fully-functioning and accomplishes its intended purposes to the best and fullest capacity.

My recent prayer to return to and remain in a first love passion with God, the Lover of my soul, is one I also pray for every believer who reads this (and even those who don't). Time and distractions can pull us away from what really matters. We were created to know the One who created us, and I don't want anything in my life to get in the way of that.

Jesus addressed the Ephesians' church in the book of Revelation regarding the loss of their first love with God. They were given a whole list of the amazing works they were doing for God-laboring, not bearing evil or growing weary, displaying patience and perseverance, and more. As a church, they were doing many admirable and noteworthy things that were making a difference.

The danger they were charged with was the fact that they were doing all of these great works but had abandoned their first love. They were shown that all of their deeds meant nothing if they did not have a first love passion in them as the driving force. They were instructed to repent and return to their first works--the first works motivated by their first love.

This is a message for all of the church, past and present. 1 Corinthians 13 lists many great works: tongues, prophecy, understanding mysteries, knowledge, faith, giving to the poor, and self-sacrificing. This is all from the same perspective that doing and having all of these wonderful gifts and services profits nothing without love. The value of anything we do outside of love is worth nothing.

I desire so strongly for my life, and any ministry God entrusts me with, to be propelled by my first love for Him. I want my words and my actions to be influenced by a love that I know deeply and personally, not one that I only hear about from others or experience secondhand. I want to remember always the way it was when I first fell in love with God. I want His love to activate all that I do, and for any work that I accomplish in His name to be an overflow of the intimate love relationship I have with Him.

A first love passion is a love that is above the love we have for anyone or anything else. Loving God is one of the two greatest commandments Jesus gives us in Scripture. He always equips us to do anything He calls us to do. The Word is our guide to understanding what it means to truly love God with all of our heart, soul, and mind. (Matthew 22:37) I want to love God with my entire being.

Psalms 26:2 and 139:23 were both penned by David, who is affectionately known as a man after God's own heart. In both verses, David's willingness and desire for God to examine his heart is one that I want to mimic in my own life. I want Him to have full access to reveal all that is happening within me, good or bad. I want Him to correct anything that doesn't please or honor Him. That means the "open" sign of my heart is always turned on for Him, because I've given Him the master key to my heart.

When we give our heart to the Lord, the process to examine, cleanse, guard, and maintain it lasts a lifetime. Surrendering our hearts is not a one and done event that happens. I believe a lot of people give their heart to God at some point in their lives, but it stops there. We have to keep ourselves open to the continual work of the Holy Spirit within us.

I desire to "live a life worthy of the Lord, fully pleasing Him, being fruitful in every good work and increasing in the knowledge of God." (Colossians 1:10) The more I know Him, the more I love Him. That love changes me and it affects everyone and everything around me as well.

I heard about a challenge people were doing some time ago where they tried to go twenty-four hours without saying anything negative, and the result was that it wasn't very easy. I think a better challenge than trying to *will* us to speak positively and avoid negative speech is to allow God to reveal and get to the root of what *causes* the negative speech to begin with. Everything we say is an overflow of what is in our heart. If the heart is taken care of, then it won't be an effort to filter what comes out of our mouth.

A really good prayer is a combination of Psalm 51:10 and Psalm 19:14. To paraphrase: God, create a clean heart within me and let the words of my mouth and the meditation of my heart please You. Praying Scripture and making it personal is powerful.

Find a group of people who have a first love passion for God. Complacency and fervency are both contagious, so catch the latter. Stay rooted and grounded in the Bible. It's God's written Word to us, so make reading it a priority. Get good mentors who can pour into your life and help you grow--those who are older in the faith and still pursuing God vigorously.

It's hard to love someone you don't know. I promise you that God is not hiding Himself from you. He wants you to know Him, so take that first step and keep going. He promises to draw near to us when we draw near to Him. (James 4:8) The only one who stops us from living a life of zeal and passion is ourselves. Shake the apathy. Shake the complacency. Shake ho-hum, monotonous living. Find your first love and enjoy a passionate, abundant life you were always created to live.

First Love Poem

Shake us from our slumber, disturb the apathy

Awake us from our sleeping, break all complacency

Fill us with unquenching zeal and blazing passion for Your name

Let us experience You in such a way we'll never be the same

Interrupt our own agendas, we lay down our man-made plans

We want to hear from Heaven, to seek Your face, not just Your hand

We declare a return to our first love, a longing to know You more

Slayin' Singlehood

We want to love You deeper than we ever have before

Boil the lukewarm waters so we're hot for You again
Ignite a burning spark inside us, fan the flame within

Keeping oil in our lamps, we will not be lulled to sleep
We silence enemy lies and serve him total vacancy

To know You and to make You known is the deepest desire of our heart
We trust fully in Your faithfulness to finish what You start

Let us see a lost and broken world both healed and returned
By the power of the gospel and the truth of Your Word

ABOUT
KHARIS PUBLISHING

KHARIS PUBLISHING is an independent, traditional publishing house with a core mission to publish impactful books, and channel proceeds into establishing mini-libraries or resource centers for orphanages in developing countries, so these kids will learn to read, dream, and grow. Every time you purchase a book from Kharis Publishing or partner as an author, you are helping give these kids an amazing opportunity to read, dream, and grow. Kharis Publishing is an imprint of Kharis Media LLC. Learn more at

https://www.kharispublishing.com.

CPSIA information can be obtained
at www.ICGtesting.com
Printed in the USA
FSHW022148310121
78202FS